Be Amazing

More Books by Paul S. Boynton

Begin with Yes: A Short Conversation that Will Change Your Life

Begin with Yes: 21-Day Companion Workbook

Commit: Transform Your Body and Your Life with the Power of Yes

Begin with Yes: At Work for You

Beginnings: A Daily Guide for Adventurous Souls

Begin with Yes, Nighttime Affirmations

Begin with Yes Action Planner

Begin with Yes, 10th Anniversary Edition

Be Amazing

Discover Your Purpose, Conquer Your
Fears, and Fulfill Your Potential

PAUL S. BOYNTON

Skyhorse Publishing

Skyhorse Publishing books may be purchased in bulk at special discounts for sales promotion, corporate gifts, fund-raising, or educational purposes. Special editions can also be created to specifications. For details, contact the Special Sales Department, Skyhorse Publishing, 307 West 36th Street, 11th Floor, New York, NY 10018 or info@skyhorsepublishing.com.

Skyhorse® and Skyhorse Publishing® are registered trademarks of Skyhorse Publishing, Inc.®, a Delaware corporation.

Visit our website at www.skyhorsepublishing.com.

10 9 8 7 6 5 4 3 2 1

Library of Congress Cataloging-in-Publication Data is available on file.

Cover design by Marko Marković

Print ISBN: 978-1-5107-4488-2
Ebook ISBN: 978-1-5107-4489-9

Printed in the United States of America

This book is dedicated to all the people who have honored me throughout the years by sharing their stories. I can think of no greater privilege than being a part of so many conversations about this beautiful journey we are all on, together. Your words are my inspiration.

Contents

Introduction

When I was younger, I didn't know what being "in the closet" meant intellectually, but emotionally, I got it loud and clear. I was well aware that I was somehow different, and that those differences were more of a problem—not a blessing. Like most kids, I was working hard to get others to love me, and I quickly learned that my best hope for that would come from *hiding* my differences, not *celebrating* them. And since that seemed to work fairly well, I stuck with this tried-and-true method with family and friends and later added coworkers, business associates, and just about everyone else who happened into my life.

Like many gay kids from my generation, I struggled with revealing myself as a complete, authentic person. It just seemed so much easier to lock such an important part of who I was far, far away, choosing to be both an outsider and an imposter to the world. I opted for this common-sense approach and turned myself into a make-believe boy, a make-believe teenager, and, ultimately, a make-believe man. I had mistakenly concluded that in order to be loved, I needed to protect others from knowing the *real* me. Looking back, I realize that this decision—made by a confused and frightened little boy— missed the simple but profound truth that to be loved as *me*, I had to *be* me.

For a long time, I thought "the closet" was invented for gay kids, but I now know that I've had plenty of company among the coat hangers. As it turned out, it wasn't just me and my gay brothers and sisters, but just about everyone I knew who had hidden a part of who they were in an attempt to please, meet expectations, and be accepted and loved. I wasn't the only little kid who had sensed that people were less interested in *who* I was and more excited about who they *wanted* me to be. And so intuitively and innocently, I cracked the closet door open looking for safety and then jumped in, full force, and slammed the door shut behind me, feeling just as scared and even more alone than ever before.

Some choose the closet rather than let others see their sensitive, vulnerable side. Some choose to play sports when all they really wanted to do was paint pictures. Many boys toughen up and learn not to cry rather than be called demeaning names. And plenty of little girls choose to be *cute* and later *sexy* rather than the bold and daring person they really are.

And we all know how many of us were taught that growing up meant abandoning our passions and our dreams to pursue practical, more financially rewarding careers. I now understand that I wasn't alone at all! The closet wasn't just for gay kids; the closet was for most kids who felt the best chance they had to be loved was to become what others wanted them to be. I now know that that closet was jam-packed with wonderful, beautiful, gifted kids of all shapes, inclinations, and sizes desperately wanting to be loved. And in the closet, it was so dark that we lost sight of how amazing we were, and before long many of us forgot that not only could we crack the door open and step outside, but we were actually meant to live amazing lives making amazing things happen.

I guess some would think that it was good news that we weren't all alone in the closet. But for me, the good news was that I found my way out. My crucial turning point was witnessing and identifying with the "coming out" episode of the Ellen DeGeneres sitcom that aired in the mid-90s. It was bold, socially provocative, and pretty gutsy of her, and it got me thinking. I didn't suddenly fling open the closet door and step out into the sunlight; I was now a grown man and things were far more complicated. I could see that even for Ellen, "coming out" meant risking a career, losing lucrative endorsement deals, and a potential shift in public perception that would very likely teach her a lesson about the risk and penalty of being *real*. And from where I stood, the lesson probably wasn't going to be very nice. That, more than anything, made me hesitate about leaving the coats behind.

But as I waited in the wings and watched Ellen wade through her own experience, I saw the power of her *authenticity*. Sure, it was messy, unpredictable, and probably pretty painful too, but it was done with such dignity and grace, and incredible self-respect. Soon, I began to feel emboldened, myself. In my case, I knew leaving the closet would be a challenge, not just for me, but for everyone who thought they knew the *real* me. "Coming out" would mean telling the truth to my loving wife, my children, friends, coworkers, and, as the CEO of a large nonprofit organization, my board of directors.

I knew from watching Ellen's journey unfold there would be very real consequences for me. But there were also so many rewards. I discovered that the *real* me was not only loving and lovable, but also so much more alive, creative, engaging, and fun to be around. I also saw so clearly that to live a passionate and purposeful life, the real me had some serious lost time to make up for!

And so, one day, I grabbed the handle, turned it slowly, eased that creaking closet door open, and stepped out into the warm light. And if you haven't already beat me to it, consider this your official invitation. If you're recognizing that you've hidden some part of yourself in the closet, here are a few things I have learned that just may help:

- Usually things we've hidden are actually some of our most unique, beautiful, and amazing attributes.
- "Coming out" late may not be better, but late beats *never,* any day.
- "Coming out" has plenty of risks and not everyone's going to like the real you, but life is filled with risks and not everyone will like you, anyway.
- Sometimes the love we want and need the most comes from *within.*
- Being yourself is not only your right, it's your reason for being here.
- What makes each of us unique is not a problem; it's an amazing blessing.
- Telling a story is easy, but telling your *authentic* story takes courage, and when we do it, we discover we are brave enough.
- And most of all, we are each born to *Be Amazing,* and although the universe will patiently wait for us to step into that circle of light, the longer we wait,

the less time we'll have to share who we're here to be.

Now, through the wonders of social media and my *Begin with Yes* book and Facebook page, so many wonderful people have come into my life. And although I may never meet them face-to-face, they've been open, willing, and brave enough to meet me, heart-to-heart. They continue to share personal stories of their own challenges and breakthroughs and how they've decided to "come out" of their own respective closets and bravely reclaim what was their birthright—their *amazingness*.

In the end, we each get to decide for ourselves the right time to "come out" and step into our own amazing potential. But I believe if you can see even a glimmer of light under the door and your hand is firmly on the handle, now just might be your moment!

If you continue reading, there will be no turning back. It's official, you are now ready to *Be Amazing*!

Be Amazing

Beyond the Door

As with many creative adventures, *Be Amazing* started with a simple thought about a remarkable experience. My partner, Mike, and I were in Walla Walla, Washington, helping friends celebrate their wedding. We were only there for the weekend and met many folks who, like us, had traveled far across the country for the festivities and a celebration of family and friends.

That Saturday morning before their exchange of vows in the park, a small group of us walked downtown to have breakfast at a restaurant that came highly recommended. There was a long line of people waiting outside, but the early fall weather was warm, and we were grateful to be together and perfectly happy to wait for the big table that would fit us all. I'll admit that although I was happy to wait, the enticing aromas and visions of pancakes smothered in maple syrup kept me on alert as each customer exited, in hopes that our party would be called next.

Finally, our table was ready. As we settled down with our menus, our server arrived with a big smile. Before even saying a word, he delivered an unexpected—but greatly appreciated—oversize apple pancake, on the house! Then he apologized for the long wait. Now, there was enough of that pancake for everyone at our table to have a substantial prebreakfast appetizer!

That gesture lifted our collective good mood even higher and made us feel welcomed and appreciated. As the coffee flowed freely, I sat back and enjoyed the corny jokes and friendly banter of old friends pleased to be together once again, on such a happy occasion.

When breakfast arrived, the apple pancake was already a happy memory. Plate after delicious plate landed on our table, setting the stage for one of the most amazing breakfasts I would ever have. There's that word: *amazing*. You'll be hearing it a lot as our conversation unfolds, and if it doesn't already describe you and your life, you're in for a treat!

Breakfast is, hands down, my favorite meal of the day, and if I had a dollar for every breakfast spot I've ever visited in my life, I'd have enough money to keep going out to breakfast as often as I wanted. You see, when it comes to breakfast spots, I'm not only a champion, I'm an *expert*! And, in my expert opinion, The Maple Counter Cafe in Walla Walla, Washington, leads the pack of my long list of favorite breakfast spots anywhere.

That October morning, this book was conceived. As I took this simple experience in, there were so many thought-provoking questions swirling through my mind: *Why were so many breakfast restaurants content with being pretty good, good enough, or just plain passable? Had managers, owners, and investors of "ok restaurants" overlooked the chance to be amazing? What exactly was it that made this restaurant in Walla Walla so amazing, and what did an amazing restaurant have to teach us about Being Amazing in other areas of our lives?* Most important, I wondered, *What does it actually take to "'Be Amazing"?*

In the weeks that followed, I began to realize that *amazing* was not just something we could all aspire to; it was something that each of us can achieve. I began to see that many people—like so many breakfast establishments—were settling for *pretty good*, or *good enough*, simply because they didn't understand that they not only had the potential, but that they were actually here on this planet to *Be Amazing*, too!

Apparently, the folks at The Maple Counter Cafe, by accident or design, had discovered the secret formula. They started with lots of smiles and genuine warmth. They welcomed special orders and made it clear that whatever a guest desired could be arranged; it was absolutely no trouble. The management was generous, as revealed by the complimentary apple pancake and generous portions. And on top of all of that, the food was simply incredibly delicious! Finally, the owners had made the decision to make real maple syrup available to anyone who wanted it—living up to the "maple" in its name. (Since I'm from New Hampshire—the land where *real* maple syrup counts, that meant a lot to me!)

Now, as amazing as all this was, it wasn't magic, and it wasn't so lofty or ambitious as to be out of reach for other restaurateurs. And it also didn't cost more or require more resources than most other restaurants had available.

I will tell you more about The Maple Center Cafe and introduce you to the owners, Kory and Rachel Nagler, but first I want to tell you more about what that breakfast experience set in motion in Walla Walla, Washington.

As I sat there enjoying the ambiance, the food, and the friendly banter at our table, I thought of my *Begin with Yes* family and all the wonderful people I am honored to share ideas and time and good vibes with every day on Facebook—now 2 million strong and growing! In that moment, I realized that this quest to *Be Amazing* was not just for restaurants or businesses, but a goal that we each can strive for individually in both our personal and professional lives. In other words, *Being Amazing* isn't just about a restaurant; it's about each one of us. It's about realizing our dreams, our goals, and our life's purpose in the most appealing way.

What I realized is that I wanted—actually *needed*—to write about my potential and your potential to *Be Amazing*, too! I'm writing this book because I believe, with all my heart, that each one of us is here to *Be Amazing*. It's not only our right; it's our responsibility. I want to help show you the way.

Since that morning, I have spent a lot of time thinking about and talking with others about what it means to *Be Amazing* and, even more important, asking, "How does *amazing* happen?" I have come to believe that there are six key qualities to strive for, and four basic steps that can move us forward. It starts with a desire to be the best that we can be in a specific area, followed by a decision to actually make it happen. Once that decision is made, we need to get specific about the key amazing qualities we need to embrace and the steps to getting there.

If this seems too simple or too easy to be true, I think you'll enjoy the rest of our conversation more than you might expect. And although you may be right about the *simple* part, the truth is, to succeed is not always easy. To make *amazing* your reality, you'll have to go beyond where most folks go. You'll need to be determined and focused, and you'll need to be prepared to have fun, too. You're about to discover that

Being Amazing is not only about a better life, it is about a more *meaningful* one, too.

So far, I've concentrated on The Maple Counter Cafe, but the truth is, we can *Be Amazing* parents, partners, spouses, employees, employers, trapeze artists, librarians, bakers, writers, painters, insurance agents, actors, dancers, or bartenders. Just listen to what's on your mind and in your heart and add that to this endless list of possibilities. Throughout this book, I'll be introducing you to people just like you, who are doing amazing things. For now, just remember that whatever your goals are, the principles I'll share will work for you.

And so now that you have the backstory and know this book's purpose, you're ready to discover what *amazing* could mean for you. So, go ahead, pour yourself another cup of coffee (or tea), and let's begin!

The Beginning

When I decided to write a new book, I also decided to stick with the conversational style that worked so well with my book *Begin with Yes*. I like to imagine we're sitting on a comfortable couch together sharing ideas, learning, and inspiring each other. I'll answer some of the typical questions I've been posed over the years from friends and strangers alike, who— like you—may be curious about the important first steps and how to best lay the groundwork for this exciting path we're walking, together. I'm incredibly excited about where you're heading and look forward to cheering from the sidelines as you make it happen!

What you will discover as our conversation unfolds is that we'll explore six qualities that will help us better understand what *amazing* is all about. Then we'll look at the four steps that will lead us toward our goals. Along the way, I will share wonderful and impactful stories that will help underscore some of the important first steps we must take. And finally, I will answer the many questions that are likely to come up as you navigate your own journey. I hope you will be able to relax into this conversation and what might be considered *work* will feel more like *fun,* and that your sense of adventure, excitement, and even your self-esteem will grow as we step forward together. Are you ready to begin?

Question: I wish I could be having breakfast with you in Walla Walla. And yes, I am ready to begin. You've already got the wheels spinning, and I'd like to hear more about what *amazing* means to you.

I wish we were out at The Maple Counter Cafe, too! Let's dig into your wonderful first question! *Amazing* is a great word that we hear and use frequently. Two of our friends, David and Michelle, were visiting us from Colorado, and as I spent time with them, I found myself doing much more listening than talking. As I listened, I began to quietly count the number of times I heard the word *amazing*. The lobster dinner was "amazing." The view from our deck was "amazing." Even our fluffy dog, Toby, was "amazing." (Thanks, Dave and Michelle. You were so right about dinner, and the view, and most of all, about Toby!)

Right now, I'd like you to begin to pay attention to how often you and others use that word, and you'll see what I mean. It seems to me that most of us like being around the adjective, *amazing*! But we seem to use the word somewhat loosely. While it's good to appreciate so much in our lives, I want to focus on what is *truly* amazing. So, I want to pose the question to you: "What truly amazing things have you bumped into in your life?"

This would be a good time for you to put the book down and make a list of some of the amazing things you've seen or experienced recently, even a while ago. I'm looking for real standouts here. Think way back if you have to: to your childhood, to faraway parts of the world, to a great evening out or a dinner you had, or maybe a show you once saw, or perhaps how someone treated you. Anything! What examples pop

into your head when you hear the word *amazing*? I'm going to pause for a moment while you make your list.

Hopefully you took a moment to start a list, and hopefully you've begun to see what a big, all-inclusive concept "amazing" really is. It's actually pretty amazing, isn't it?

Let me share with you a few of my own thoughts. For me, *Being Amazing* starts when we're engaged with our lives, passionate about what we're doing, and excited about the things we are creating. What you'll discover as we move forward is that *Being Amazing* is much easier—even effortless—whenever we are passionate about what we're doing. But that's just the start; it still requires careful follow-through.

Now, I'm betting you've already figured out that what we're passionate about is closely tied to our purpose. And please keep in mind that most of us have more than one purpose and more than one passion, too. That's good news, because we don't just get to be amazing in one area of our lives. We have the potential to *Be Amazing* in all kinds of ways.

But let's not get ahead of ourselves just yet. Let's begin by focusing on a single area that's important to you.

When I first told Kory and Rachel about my experience at The Maple Counter Cafe and how it had inspired me to write a new book, they were incredibly excited and supportive. They were more than willing to share their secrets! Rachel said, "From the very beginning, what we were determined to do is create a space that 'smiles on the world' (a phrase coined by Kory's dad)—a place where both our customers and staff feel safe and cared for. We truly believe that the love and positivity we put into the restaurant and share with our employees are the keys to our success."

She continued: "What we have tried to create at the Cafe is a family—one that includes employees and customers. One thing that helped in the early years was a staff-initiated 'family meal' every Sunday night. We'd get together at one another's houses or other restaurants in town. Nothing made me prouder than when I heard everyone leaving after a long Sunday serving breakfast, saying, 'See you later tonight!' That we co-created an occasion like this seems very powerful."

I'm sure that you can feel the passion and sincerity in Rachel's words. Rachel and Kory both know that *Being Amazing* means doing your personal best (which is much different from being "better than"), and it's also about being passionate, feeling alive, and being fully engaged. *Being Amazing* means caring deeply about the outcome of an endeavor; it means being unwilling to settle for *pretty good* or just *good enough*, and it's also about having a positive impact on the people you meet along the way.

Let me share a few other things I learned from Kory and Rachel. Kory told me that an amazing restaurant isn't just about the food. Good food helps, but *how you make people feel is paramount*. "Kindness is everything," he said. "It really is that simple." He went on to explain that kindness needs to originate *from within*. "A genuine attempt to connect with strangers and acquaintances alike allows us to share in the greater human experience."

Kory believes there's a direct relationship between loving what you do and doing it well. "If you are not happy in your life, you will ultimately wear it at work. People can sense this, and it will diminish your ability to lift people up around you and create that magic that makes you and your business amazing. Being 'truly happy' does not mean everything in your life is perfect or just how you'd like it to be. Rather, I believe true happiness can exist in tandem with struggle and sadness. We tend to think of things as either/or, when in fact, more often we are called to make room for feelings to coexist. It's learning how to allow or *choose* happiness despite the struggles that makes having an 'amazing' life possible."

Kory and Rachel are amazing people doing amazing things, and when I asked them if they'd be willing to share a pancake recipe from The Maple Counter Cafe, they laughed and said, "We'd love to!"

Swedish Pancakes

This recipe makes several pancakes and can be held in the refrigerator for up to five days. At The Maple Counter Cafe, the pancake is cooked on a thermostatically controlled griddle at 360 degrees. When you use a pan on a stove, there is a larger margin of error when determining exact cook time. The first side of the pancake should be a golden brown, while the second side will remain pale.

1½ quarts water
1 oz. powdered skim milk
Whisk together well and then continue adding:
1 lb. flour
3½ oz. baker's sugar
3½ oz. salt
Whisk together and then continue adding:

¾ cups peanut oil
Whisk together well and then continue adding:
5 eggs stiffly whipped (preferably in a stand mixer for several
    minutes until the eggs resemble a meringue)
Whisk together one last time.

Lightly coat a cast-iron skillet (or a nonstick pan) with but-
ter and heat to medium. Before pouring batter onto the heated
surface, be sure to whisk it vigorously. Pour into the center of
the pan slowly and allow the batter to spread to the edge of the
pan. Carefully flip the pancake once it has set up and continue
cooking on the other side for half the time it cooked on the first
side.

    Serve with whipped butter and your choice of jarred lingon-
berries or warm maple syrup.

    I hope a few of you will try the recipe, and if you're ever in
the Walla Walla area and would like to meet Rachel and Kory
and get a tour of *The Maple Counter Cafe*, here's how to find
them to make that possible: www.maplecountercafe.com.

Question: It seems like we've covered a lot of ground, and I'm excited about beginning my own amazing journey. Could you tell me more about those six *Amazing* qualities and give me an example or two?

I am glad you're excited and you're right to ask for more specifics. For now, I will use examples from The Maple Counter Cafe to help explain the qualities, but as our conversation unfolds, you will begin to see how easy it is to apply these same attributes to all sorts of personal and professional goals.

Be Amazing Quality One: Offer unexpected acts of generosity, kindness, and other thoughtful behaviors.

The unanticipated and complimentary giant pancake appetizer at The Maple Counter Cafe is a perfect example of this first quality. Bringing us a free pancake didn't cost much, but the impression it made was priceless. As brand-new customers, we discovered that we were at an establishment that didn't take our wait-time lightly. What's more, they wanted to start our meal off right with a genuine welcome. That pancake signaled that we were going to be treated with generosity and kindness. This thoughtful gesture set the tone for the rest of our time at The Maple Counter Cafe. It even inspired a book!

Looking beyond the Cafe, think about an employer who gives an extra holiday to hard-working employees. Or a friend who is generous with her time, stopping to listen to you sort out a problem you're dealing with. Imagine a grandfather who remembers to have your favorite candy bar in his coat pocket always at the ready, or a baker who offers a customer a dozen cookies for a local bake sale without even being asked.

What's especially great is that you'll discover that that old adage is true: It's better to give than to receive. You'll have as much fun doing it as your recipient will feel on the receiving end—maybe even more so. This is truly a win-win proposition. And you'll discover that generosity sets goodwill in motion and that the happiness you create almost always finds its way back to you.

Be Amazing Quality Two: Don't necessarily strive for being the best but do strive to be the very best you can be.

While the pancake, and indeed all the food at The Maple Counter Cafe, was exceptional, it was the cumulative effect of delicious food, superior service, friendly staff, and the homey environment that added up to such a memorable experience. Rachel and Kory understood that it wasn't just about the pancakes, but it started with that. My morning at their café wouldn't have been so special if the pancakes—even the free ones—had been mediocre or even average. But if they'd been spectacular and the service had been brusque, you wouldn't be reading this book right now.

So, it's not about being the best dancer or potter or bank teller, but it *is* about always delivering your best. And the way you deliver it matters.

There is a Zen saying that flowers don't compare themselves with other flowers, they just bloom. *Being Amazing* isn't about being better than everyone else, but it is about each of us blooming in magnificent, powerful, and beautiful ways, almost certainly in a garden full of beautiful blooms.

Being your best requires establishing goals and then pushing beyond them. It means learning, practice, trial and error, and then even more practice. It's a lot of work, but don't let that scare you. It's most certainly worth it, and the satisfaction you'll find along the way makes it easier to do than you might think.

Be Amazing Quality Three: Have an intention that becomes a narrative—even if it's only one sentence long.

As Rachel said, "From the very beginning, we set out to create a space that 'smiles on the world' (a phrase coined by Kory's dad). We wanted a place where both customers and staff felt safe and cared for. We truly believe that the love and positivity we put into the restaurant and share with our employees are the keys to our success."

This basic and heartfelt intention actually was their fundamental organizing principle. This core belief, or mantra, declared, "Here is what we are about; welcome to our version of *Being Amazing.*"

At The Moore Center, a New Hampshire nonprofit where I serve as CEO, we provide community-based services to men and women with intellectual disabilities as well as seniors who simply want to keep their independence while remaining in their own homes. Our intention and mission is: "Creating opportunities for others to have a good life." We aim to level the playing ground by creating partnerships with others in the community that are mutually beneficial and allow those "opportunities" to emerge. One major factor that reinforces my belief in what's possible is being surrounded by optimistic, hopeful, daring, hardworking, lovable, and loving families, clients, staff, community partners, and volunteers who work with us to achieve amazing results. Being surrounded by amazing people doing amazing things fuels my desire to help others see their own potential to be amazing, and I hope you are beginning to catch a glimmer of what might be possible for you. My challenge for you is pretty simple, absolutely possible, and completely amazing, too.

So be that receptionist whom people can't wait to see first thing in the morning. Be the MRI tech who knows how scary medical tests can be and who goes out of their way to calm those nervous patients to help them feel safe, supported, and reassured. Or strive to be the partner who has decided to love unconditionally—even during the challenging times. Be the baker who hears every day that his cupcakes are the best, or the dog walker who loves the dogs in her care as much as her own beloved Goldendoodle she happily walks every morning.

As our conversation unfolds, we will be looking at what you want your life to be about. What we discover together will soon become the music you'll dance to. I believe with all my heart that once you get started, your life will never be the same.

Be Amazing Quality Four: Be as accommodating as possible.

If you remember, we had a bit of a wait to get into The Maple Counter Cafe. We were alongside friends, which made the wait that much more endurable, but it became even easier once Rachel started coming outside every few minutes to let waiting customers know that they hadn't been forgotten, that things were moving along, and that our turn was just around the corner.

The fact that so many people were also waiting made the restaurant even more desirable and reminded me that what we were waiting for inside was probably going to be pretty special. And then those happy, smiling, satisfied faces leaving the restaurant also kept our mood and expectations high all the while as our bellies rumbled.

Once we were seated, this sense of accommodation continued. First the complimentary pancake arrived, then the cheerful and friendly staff kept our coffee cups filled as we ultimately learned that "special orders" that deviated from the menu were not just tolerated, but welcomed. This was not a "no substitutions" enterprise. It was a "tell us what you want" business that put their customers first.

You'll have plenty of chances to add this quality on your own amazing journey. You may be the parent who puts down his computer or phone to play a game *right now* rather than *in a minute*. You may open your beauty salon one Saturday morning for a customer with a haircut disaster. Or a Lyft driver who helps a passenger load luggage into the trunk. Being accommodated can be a positive game changer for many simply because we aren't used to it. A little tender loving care goes a long way.

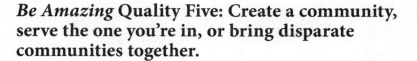

Be Amazing Quality Five: Create a community, serve the one you're in, or bring disparate communities together.

Again, Rachel's casual comments illustrate this so beautifully. "What we have tried to create at The Maple Counter Cafe is a family—both a family of employees and a family of customers." This desire for community is actually a profound statement of what they value, what they want their restaurant to express, and what they have created.

And although the employee tradition of hanging out together Sunday nights (not because they had to, but because they *wanted* to) was not something we knew about at the time, we could feel the camaraderie, and that just simply felt unusual and very, very good. As customers, we couldn't help but sense the family culture of the Cafe, and we were just happy to be a small part of it.

As an amazing parent, we get to create community with our families and then an extended community with the important people in our children's lives. We create community when we have pizza delivered for our employees every once in a while or when we remember a customer's first name and introduce them to someone else also waiting for their pooch at the dog groomer's.

Creating community does require a little extra energy and attention, but the result is what most of us are looking for. We want to belong and feel part of something, and when we ourselves can make that happen, so much the better.

Be Amazing Quality Six: Be authentic about and focused on things you feel passionate about.

This last quality is actually a dealmaker. All that we have talked about has seemed to be focused on a business or, more specifically, a restaurant. But I hope you've been reading between the lines and have sensed that what we're really talking about is much more personal. It's about enthusiasm, engagement, hard work, and passion. Kory and Rachel didn't have to continue their family's tradition of hospitality, but they followed that dream because that's what they felt called to do. If asked, they'd probably say, "We were just intuitively doing what felt right to us." And I would quietly point out, "Yes, and look how far that has taken you."

This last quality is an invitation to each of you reading this book. As you explore, discover, or rediscover the things that make your heart beat just a little faster, you will actually be choosing your own amazing journey. And although we have Kory and Rachel and The Maple Counter Cafe to thank for the inspiration, what will happen next will be dictated by you and your dreams.

As we move forward, I'll have more stories to share, but our focus will be helping you pursue these six amazing qualities for yourself, your business, your life, and wherever your heart's desire is leading you.

I look forward to creating a community of amazing grandparents, trombone players, hair stylists, real estate agents, matchmakers, hospice volunteers, teachers, baristas, homemakers, pilots, caregivers, artists, physicians, social workers, coaches, landscapers, or whatever else you can think of that resonates with and calls out to you. We are going to travel to remarkable places together, and I am just as excited to see what's going to happen next as you are. In fact, I can hardly wait!

I hope this review of *Be Amazing* qualities has you excited with all kinds of ideas floating through your mind. These qualities are intended to get that positive energy flowing but not intended to be restrictive or to slow you down. Not every quality will emerge in clearly definable ways, and I hope that you won't use them as a checklist to verify or confirm your own results as you move forward. Instead, use them as touchstone and reminders, so if you get stuck or need encouragement or ideas, revisit this list and see what new ideas pop into your head. And since that phrase "pop into your head" just popped into my mine—please do invite and celebrate that heart-opening and creative energy you'll begin to experience more and more as you head into the unknown with me by your side, because that's the life force that keeps you moving and makes you smile, too!

Oh, one last thing before we move on. I'm often asked, "Why should I *Be Amazing*?" The answer is pretty simple. Because you *can* be. Because that's why you're here. Because the world needs more amazing people doing amazing things. And most of all, because it's one of the greatest feelings you will ever have!

Here, let me hold the door open for you. Exciting things are just outside!

Question: I am pretty excited and have a few amazing possibilities beginning to take shape in my mind. I'd love to get started, but first I'd like to hear another story or two for inspiration. Could you provide a few more?

I'm happy to hear that your mind is spinning with your own amazing potential. It's funny, ever since I started looking for amazing people doing amazing things, I've discovered all kinds of amazing stories, and, unfortunately, I have also witnessed too many examples that illustrate the "good enough for now" approach to life, too. There will be plenty of folks who will settle for less, but I am pretty sure that you want more in your life and you're ready to do what it takes to make that happen.

In answer to your request, here's a story of a Lyft driver named Todd who clearly wasn't willing to settle.

Like Uber and several other similar startups, Lyft is a fairly young company that allows you to order local transportation via an app on your phone. It's like having access to your own personal taxi service with convenience and lower fares all part of the deal. I love Lyft and use it all the time.

One reason it works so well is that the passengers get to review the drivers and the drivers rate the passengers, too. When you are booking your ride, you get to see how your driver has been rated by former passengers, and the driver gets to see how former drivers have rated you. This two-way evaluation keeps everyone on their very best behavior.

The other day, I arranged for a ride after a conference, and within a couple minutes my car arrived. The driver's name was Todd. Once we exchanged greetings and pleasantries, we continued the conversation as he drove me to my destination. As we chatted amiably, I told him how impressed I was that he had gotten the highest possible five-star rating. Todd smiled and thanked me for mentioning it. Then he said something that really caught my attention. "Ever since I started with this company, all I ever really wanted was to be an amazing driver. I love this job, and I appreciate hearing that people have noticed my enthusiasm and are appreciating me for it."

Now, even though our ride was going to be pretty short, he had, as you might imagine, my full attention. And so, I asked a few questions to discover how those amazing qualities were showing up for him. Here's what I learned:

The first thing I noticed when I got in Todd's car was how comfortable, clean, and ready it was. It even smelled nice. There were magazines neatly tucked inside the sleeve on the backside of the front seat, and the air conditioning was on. Todd greeted me by name (the phone app shares first names) and flashed me a genuine, engaging smile. He was a big man with a deep voice and a great laugh, and he was instantly likable. Todd seemed really glad to see me, reminded me to fasten my seat belt, and then asked if I wanted a small bottle of water. These were fairly simple, inexpensive gestures, but in all my Lyft rides taken thus far, this was the first time some-one had offered me a bottle of water.

As we chatted, I learned that Todd loved his job because he got to meet "mostly nice" people from all over the world. He felt that was not only an honor and a learning experience, but it was also a lot of fun, too. He never once mentioned being the best Lyft driver out there, but he did tell me that he had decided that if he was going to do this work, he was going to make it meaningful by being the very best driver he could be. I could guess that doing his best meant being prompt and friendly, keeping his car superclean and comfortable, and making people feel welcome in "his" city. I found myself telling him about my work, my family, and my visit to San Francisco, and by the time the ride was over, I felt like I had met a new friend.

If there was anyone intentional about *Being Amazing*, it was Todd. Again, this wasn't very complicated, and he didn't need a focus group or even a mission statement to make his goal crystal clear. Within minutes, I knew what this man's calling was, and I knew he took his work very seriously. As such, his life was made even more meaningful.

Todd asked where I was having dinner and wondered if I needed any restaurant suggestions. As we got closer to my drop-off, he asked if there was an exact location that worked best for me. And when we arrived, he made sure to pull over and park to make it easy for me to exit safely. "Check to make sure you have your phone and everything else, Paul," he said with that great, infectious smile of his, and he reached his hand out to greet mine for a farewell handshake.

I realized later in the day that when two strangers share a short, simple car ride, community is created. And although it's highly unlikely that our paths will cross again, thanks to Todd, I felt better about being in an unfamiliar city and had even made a new *Begin with Yes* friend on my Facebook page. In case you're reading this, Todd, thanks for that amazing ride!

Now let me tell you another pretty simple but extraordinary story. This one's about a woman I met many years ago.

Her name is Donna and she's in her late eighties and she's one of the most amazing friends I have ever had.

I don't think Donna woke up one day and decided she wanted to be an amazing friend, but that's pretty much what the focus of her life has been. And even though this was never a deliberate choice, the amazing qualities we've been exploring couldn't be more evident in how she approaches life.

Let me tell you a bit about this wonderful lady. The first thing that comes to mind is Donna's incredible ability to remember birthdays and anniversaries. Sometimes you'll receive a card in the mail, other times a phone message, and more often than not a small, thoughtful, "dollar store" gift.

If you happen to run into Donna at an event or restaurant, her face lights up as if a long-lost and dearly loved relative were surprising her with an unannounced visit. She is quick to envelop you in a hug, will sometimes hold your hand as you chat, and—I kid you not—will sometimes tear up when she tells you how glad she is to see you. Generous, kind, and thoughtful behaviors just come naturally to Donna, and, like so many others in our community, I feel blessed to have her grace my life.

I am always telling Donna that she is the nicest person I know, and she just laughs and scolds me for exaggerating. Not only isn't she trying to be "the best," she really doesn't quite grasp just how wonderful she is. I don't know this for a fact and perhaps one day I will ask her, but here's what I think. When Donna was a child, her parents must have taught her that goodness and kindness were important and natural traits to be shared. They must have seen the light around her, and I bet they simply encouraged her to let that light shine!

She puts the needs of others first, not because she doesn't have a strong ego or a clear sense of self-respect, but because she enjoys seeing others feel just as good about themselves as she feels about herself. She never comes across as a doormat or as someone with boundary issues or low self-esteem. Rather, she shows up as someone who just loves people and wants to make the world a bit brighter. If we could visualize the ripples of goodness set in motion by this amazing woman, we would see no end to the goodness she creates every day.

Donna also loves bringing people together. There have been times when she has literally taken my hand and put it in the hand of someone new she wanted me to meet. By example, she encourages folks like me to slow down and enjoy life a bit, to laugh, and to tell one another stories. I am fairly certain Donna isn't actively thinking about how important it is to build a sense of community, but I am absolutely certain she's living it!

There's one more thing I want to share about Donna. Most of us know when someone is acting nice but not feeling nice. We know a disingenuous smile when we see it, and we also know when it's the real deal. We can sense when people love us for who we are versus using us for what we have or what we might be able to do. We know authenticity when we see it. And we know passion when we feel it. I wish you could meet Donna, and I am even thinking of ways I might be able to make that happen using social media. But for now, trust me: Donna has mastered the art of being an authentic, passionate, amazing friend!

Question: I'm beginning to recognize or remember some of the amazing people in my own life. Maybe someday you will write a book just telling stories about all the amazing people you've met. But right now, I'm ready to take that leap into *amazing* myself. I'm not sure where to start, and I am wondering why people, well actually I am wondering why *I* have been so reluctant to reach for more and to expect more from myself. I wonder what has been standing in my way?

Thanks for the kind words and the next book idea, too. I am so glad you're ready to begin. You are about to discover that it's easier than you might think. In just a short time, I'm going to give you a few simple steps you can take to get started, and I am really looking forward to hearing where you're headed. And who knows? If I ever do write a book telling stories about amazing people, your story could be one I'll be telling! But first, let's back up just a bit and take a look at some of the common realities some of us have that may stand in our way.

Here is a list of some of the typical challenges or realities that people have told me were holding them back:

I'm too old.
Too tired.
Too young, too out of shape, too busy.
It's too difficult.
It's not the right time.
It's too late for me.
I don't have a degree. I don't have the right degree.
I don't have any money. I don't have enough money.

I have too many family responsibilities.

I have no energy, no time, no talent, and no support system.

And the list goes on and on and on. If your favorite isn't here, go ahead and add it. I think you get the idea—we are creative people and have used our imagination or our thoughts to proclaim all the reasons why we haven't pursued our dreams. Many of us haven't imagined we could be amazing because no one ever told us that it was not only possible, but actually it was our birthright.

Now, you may be thinking that I am not being realistic or practical. If your dream is to be an amazing nurse, then you're right, you do need a degree. And getting a degree takes time and it takes money, too. And you may also already be working hard, and you may, in fact, be tired. Becoming an amazing nurse can be a complicated and long-term journey, or it may not even make sense for all kinds of reasons. And if that's where you end up after being bold and willing to take risks, then I have some ideas that will help, and you can be sure there are still many reasons for you to be excited and hopeful and hanging on tight to things you feel passionate about.

I promise to circle back to this issue shortly, but for now, know that I actually want you to be realistic and gentle with yourself as you plan your own amazing journey. But I don't want you to give up too easily or throw in the towel unnecessarily, because I have seen first-hand people like you and me who have done what they once thought were impossible things. And here's how I think they managed that.

They somehow discovered a powerful truth that this list of roadblocks is more often really just a list of things we need to deal with, not a list of things that have to derail us. Sure, they sound like really good excuses, and I have used a few of them myself, but the simple truth is, very often they're just excuses. Of course, many of these challenges may be legitimate and they may require workarounds or even rerouting, but at the end of the day, they're usually not the end of the road.

When all is said and done, I've discovered that there are really only two fundamental things that are standing in our way, and neither one is on the list above. The first thing standing in our way is *our thoughts*, and the second is our *unwillingness to take action*.

Let's spend a few minutes right now talking about *our thoughts*, because I think you will see a few things that will change how you look at the world.

To begin with, it's not really that we're *too old*, or *too busy* or too anything else. The problem is we've chosen to think and then believe these things. And the reason this distinction is so important is that our thoughts are very, very powerful. In fact, our thoughts actually create our realities.

If we think we're too old, we are, in fact, too old.

If we think we're too busy, we are, in fact, too busy.

We are actually creating our realities with our thoughts. And when we understand that, we begin to see that if we can change our thoughts, we can actually change our realities, too.

As a side note, keep in mind that everyone else is also creating their realities with their own thoughts. No wonder when we are working with others, we often find it so hard to see someone else's perspective, and it's no wonder that it can be such a challenge to find common ground and solutions to the challenges that may be facing us.

Question: If I am hearing you right, you are suggesting that the things we think are holding us back are really just our thoughts?

Exactly. What we think is reality is really just *our* reality, not *the* reality. Imagine you and a few mutual friends are hanging out at the beach on a typical New Hampshire summer day. It's almost ninety degrees, and there's not a cloud in the sky and barely a breeze, either. I, myself, am not particularly comfortable in direct sunshine, and I remark, "Wow, it's hot out!" as I open up the umbrella and reach for the sunscreen and some more ice for my lemonade.

But you happen to love the beach and its accompanying sunshine (don't forget the sunblock!), and you've not only waited all winter for a day like this, but this is your perfect day! We might laugh when we discover our different perspectives because we have both described the very same day, just in different terms. I am uncomfortably warm and can't wait for things to cool down, and you hope the rest of the week is just like today.

Is it an uncomfortably hot day or a perfect beach day? The truth is it's 90 degrees and the sun is shinning. The rest is simply our *spin*.

This is a simple illustration about how we create reality with our thoughts, but it becomes more meaningful when we realize we are creating our *spin* all the time. Our thoughts don't change the facts or what's real, but our thoughts do create how we experience the facts. And this gets even more problematic for us, because we begin to think that how we percieve the world is how the world is. And then we take it a step further: we assume that everyone sees the world the very same way we do. We decide that our view is the real one or the right one and suspect that our view surely must be aligned with everyone else's.

And if everyone else is doing the same thing with their own perceptions, it's no wonder we have conflicts and arguments about what may or may not need to be fixed and how to fix it. And it's no wonder that relationships of all kinds have all kinds of unintended and often unnecessary challenges as we navigate though these conflicting realities.

Here'a a story that illustrates the power of our thoughts in a somewhat embarrasing, personal way. (I don't mind sharing because it's kind of funny, too!) A few years ago, at the start of a wonderful romance, my new live-in partner had taken a trip back to the West Coast to visit his family over the holidays. As I prepared for our reunion when he returned, I thought it would be a romantic gesture to get a single red rose to put bedside. So on my way home from work, I stopped at a grocery store and headed to the floral department. I told the clerk that I wanted to buy "a single red rose." She went into the cooler and brought out an armful of roses and told me I could take my pick.

Noticing that some of the leaves were starting to turn brown and wanting to get *the* perfect rose, I put some real energy into finding that one special long-stem-beauty. I finally made my selection, and she gingerly attached one of those small water vials to the stem, added some greens, wrapped it in a white floral paper to protect it from the cold, stapled a packet of plant food to the package, and sent me on the way to the register. When I got home, I filled a small vase with water, cut the very hard stem so it could absorb the water, and dutifully added the plant food as instructed. Then I arranged the rose and the greens and placed my beautiful bouquet on the bedside table. And you'll be glad to know, it was a hit!

Almost two weeks later, I was putting some clothes away in another room, and I heard a puzzled voice call out, "Why on Earth did you put a fake rose in water?"

"What?" I yelled back.

So I marched in and looked for myself, and I discovered not only was the rose fake—it was a pretty bad fake at that. You see, for very logical and understandable reasons, thinking it was real, I picked out a fake rose from an armful of fake roses, had it wrapped to protect it from the winter outside, brought it home, cut off the very hard plastic stem, put it in a vase with water, added plant food, and then, without questioning for even a minute, watched it stay exactly the same for almost two weeks. All because I had the thought in my mind that it was a real rose!

Pretty powerful thought, huh? (I should add that I am convinced that the high school student clerk believed the roses were real, too. My guess is, someone inadvertently placed a display into the cooler and she just grabbed the first red roses she saw. Either way, I think the Universe was playing a pretty good joke on us all.)

Here's another story that might first make you smile and then make you wonder if you may be doing something similar. Let me tell you about a guy that I see at the gym most mornings. A while back, I passed him on the way to the treadmill and asked him how his day was. He didn't miss a beat and quickly answered: "Mondays suck." I knew immediately that this exchange would be a perfect story for my book but also knew this was a sad way for anyone to begin a new week.

This man had horrible Mondays, not because Mondays were horrible, but because he decided for himself that's what Mondays were going to be like. I saw him the next day, and I just couldn't resist asking him about his Monday! And here's what he said: "Well, at least it's over." Pretty depressing, huh?

Now let's do the math. We're not just talking about wasting one perfectly good day. We're talking about wasting 52 Mondays a year! I needed my calculator to discover that if he lives to be 75, that's 3,900 days! A good ten full years of his life, all ruined by a powerful, but totally unnecessary negative thought.

The last time I saw this guy, he was literally glowing. I asked him how he was doing. "It's Friday. The weekend's here," he replied. This is a man who seems to live for the weekends. So although his Mondays, and now I think his Tuesdays, Wednesdays, and Thursdays, also are awful, at least he's having fun on the weekend!

Once again, the truth is our individual reality, how we experience the world, is not so much about our circumstances, but about how we anticipate, react, or respond to whatever comes our way. Simply said, each morning we wake up, brush our teeth, and begin our day. And just like the guy at the gym, more often than not, we get to create our reality. And since we're creating it, doesn't it make more sense to create realities that move us forward, rather than realities that hold us back? And doesn't it make more sense to create realities that help us feel better, rather than realities that bring us down and make us feel bad? And doesn't it make sense to think more about a world where

possibilities exist, even when things get challenging, than a world full of imposssible roadblocks and dead ends?

If the man at the gym understood this and said to himself, "Oh boy, it's Monday! A brand new week filled with possibilities," he'd instantly gain ten more years of happiness.

Lots of people have written or talked about the power of our thoughts. The writer Thoreau wrote, "It's not so much what we look at, it's what we see." If we see roadblocks, we stand back. If we see excuses, we find a way to avoid the challenges. However, if we see possibilities, we keep moving forward.

Author Marianne Williamson said, "You can see the glass as half-full or half-empty, but whatever you see, you're going to get more of it!" If your glass is half-empty, you'll see roadblocks. If your glass is half-full, you'll begin looking for solutions.

Here's another one I love. Author Anaïs Nin wrote, "We don't see things as they are, we see things as we are." If we see ourselves as out of luck, we are likely to stay put. If we see our potential, we will be eager to seek out opportunities and step into the unknown where amazing awaits.

And even our very first First Lady Martha Washington weighed in when she wrote in a letter to a friend, "The greatest part of our happiness, or misery, depends on our disposition and not on our circumstances."

Henry David, Marianne, Anaïs and Martha were all saying pretty much the same thing: with our thoughts, we actually create our realities. In other words, we choose how to perceive the world, and then, that's what the world becomes.

This misunderstanding all started when we were kids, and by the time we got to be adults, we had mistakenly convinced ourselves that our view of the world is how things actually were, when in fact, it's really just our view and not a view that always encouraged us to think creatively and to move forward easily!

But that's good news, because once we realize what we've done, we can reconsider. We can change our realities by changing our thoughts. It takes a little practice, but we can actually retrain our minds to view the world differently. I know that we have spent a bit of time on this side journey, but you'll be discovering how important it will be as we move toward *amazing*. I wanted you to be prepared and ready to deal with and challenge some realities that await, and now you are.

Question: I am feeling slightly "guilty as charged" and wonder, do you have any suggestions about how I can reprogram my mind and create realities that serve me better and make my goals more achievable?

The good news is, reprograming is really just retraining our minds to open up to alternative views or thoughts. It's a chance to get creative and to see possibilities instead of brick walls. And I can promise you that as you practice, you will get better at it, and *Being Amazing* will become more likely, more rapid, and even easier than you thought. The basic new skill you will want to learn is what I call *reframing*. Here's a story that will show you how that works.

A couple years ago, Mike and I were out for a car ride with no real destination in mind. We ended up in a rural area a few hours away from our home, and we were discovering new places and seeing a part of the state that was new to us. As we drove by a house with many additions, I absentmindedly commented, "Look at that ugly house." Almost instantly, before Mike could even reply, I knew what I had done. Using words and thoughts and my own personal likes and dislikes, I had labeled someone else's house as "ugly."

This house was actually someone else's home. Someone else had created this house, was paying the mortgage, was mowing the lawn, had painted the shed, and was raising a family there. What I had called an ugly house was actually a beautiful home. And who was I to critique someone's home? How did it serve me to call it *ugly*?

Quickly, I reframed what I had said by saying, "the style of that house doesn't appeal to me." The house hadn't changed one bit, but my thoughts had. I laugh as I write this and think of our own home filled with books, paintings, and mementos that have a special meaning to us. Some might say it's "cluttered," but we think it's a really cozy, warm, and love-filled home.

Since that ride, I have been more intentional about reframing my thoughts—it's really become more like a game, and it's enhanced my ability to be more creative, more open, and more willing to see possibilities. It also has the bonus of making me less judgmental and more likable and easier to be around. When my thoughts about the house changed, the house changed, too. As your thoughts about your current and potential reality expand, what's possible for you will, too. Practice will help, and the change you create will be, shall I say, amazing!

Listen to what Thoreau had to say about retraining our minds: "As a single footstep will not make a path on the earth, so a single thought will not make a pathway in the mind. To make a deep physical path, we walk again and again. To make a deep mental path, we must think over and over the kind of thoughts we wish to dominate our lives."

And one more thing, before we move on: once you understand how much of your reality you are creating with your mind, you will never return to the place where you feel totally powerless. And from this new place of being more powerful, your quest to *Be Amazing* will now quite naturally become part of your new reality.

All that to say, let's not be like the man in the gym! Let's remember that our thoughts are powerful and we are taking these thoughts in and treating them as truths.

Question: I am so anxious to really get into and onto my own amazing journey, but you said there were really two things that hold us back. What's the second thing?

Thanks for the reminder and for keeping me on track. The second thing that gets in our way is our reluctance to just roll up our sleeves. Most of us have been told, "Attitude is everything," but the truth is, attitude will only get us so far. Having dreams and goals and a positive attitude is a great way to create focus and gives us a sense of hope, but taking action is really the only way we'll ever move from hoping something amazing happens to actually making something amazing happen.

And once again, misusing the power of our thoughts, we've made taking action way too complicated, way too big, and way too overwhelming, and we often find ourselves simply standing still or stuck. And the way to get unstuck is to simply refocus from the overwhelming to the next small step and begin putting one foot in front of the other. I will have more to say about those small steps in a bit, but for now take a moment to just enjoy the thought that you are on your way to amazing, too!

Question: I get this and actually find it liberating, yet I also think some of our challenges are real and "rolling up our sleeves" isn't going to cut it. And on behalf of the older person who wanted to be an amazing nurse, I actually want to push back here a bit. The need for a degree, the lack of financial resources, and no time sure seem like real problems. Right?

You are so right, and your questions deserve honest, straight-talking answers. Here are a few of my thoughts on dealing with real challenges. First of all, don't give up too easily. Don't believe you can't afford it until you've had an honest conversation with a financial advisor at a nearby school. If you're too tired, don't give up until you have really looked at what you're doing that you could stop doing while you go back to school.

When we are feeling *stuck*, we need to dig deeper, not give up. I truly respect you for pushing back but also want to encourage you to also try pushing through. Big dreams don't often come easily. Success doesn't usually fall out of the sky and gently land at our feet. If after an honest effort to challenge reality, you still feel stalled, let me show how amazing dreams or goals can be reframed and can still be reached.

When I was a kid, more than anything, I wanted to be an actor—not a movie star, mind you, but an amazing Broadway musical performer. And it wasn't just a passing fancy; it was part of my *spirit blueprint*, and it never went away. Now, I had some challenges to deal with. I lived in a small town in New Hampshire and I didn't have any friends who shared my interests and there weren't any actual theaters or theater people around me I could learn from or be inspired by. I didn't have parents who could understand, much less *imagine* that was a possibility, and I gradually accepted their verdict. In addition, I couldn't sing on-key to save my life! So, as the years passed, I learned how to package that dream up and store it away. But it didn't actually get buried too deeply. (Thank goodness for that!)

I went to college, got a degree in social work, got married, started a family, focused on my career and life and paying the bills. Every once in a while, I would take the dream back out and imagine what *could have been*.

When my own kids were in elementary school, I unpacked that dream a bit and started a small community theater for children and adults in the small town where we lived. It was called *The Charmingfare Theater*, and although we started small with a Christmas pageant, before long we were producing major musicals with huge casts, a full orchestra, big (by most community theater standards) scary budgets, and almost two hundred neighbors fully engaged in helping to make the impossible happen. It was amazing. The passion was unleashed, and I suddenly discovered that in a small town in New Hampshire, I was surrounded by folks who loved theater, too. I share this as an example of how I took my dream to be an amazing Broadway actor and turned into a dream of being an amazing community theater director.

And I didn't stop there! A few years ago, I convinced Michael and a couple of friends to take tap dancing lessons with me. Our teacher, Sandi Duncan (not the one you're thinking of), was also a big believer in making dreams come true, and we had a ball. I didn't turn out to be an amazing tap dancer, but I did become an amazing fun-seeking tap dancing student. Every once in a while, I post a video of me tapping and laughing and having the time of my life on the *Begin with Yes* Facebook page to inspire others to reframe and follow their dreams, too.

But let's say you're that 75-year-old man or woman grounded in reality and your dream of being an amazing nurse is really not in the cards. Don't give up! I urge you—actually beg you—to unpack that dream and try reframing your passion into something else that might work for a 75-year-old with a yet-to-be-fulfilled mission. Maybe you could be an amazing volunteer at your local hospital, or a part-time receptionist at a doctor's office. Or perhaps you could work part-time as an amazing helpline responder. I encourage you to use your imagination and even ask friends to help brainstorm ideas. I have never met a dream that couldn't be reimagined, and if you have really tried to think of some way to move forward and you keep coming up empty, send me a note and let me see what I can come up with! Remember this: if you find yourself totally unable to pursue a specific dream right now or ever, don't pack it up, but reframe it and make it happen.

PS: I recently spoke to a group, and, after chatting with a few folks, an elderly woman waited to speak with me. She shared she had always wanted to be an amazing pianist, but for whatever reason, it just never happened. However, a while back, she had started taking piano lessons, and after I shared my story, she decided she was going to be the most amazing 86-year-old piano student possible. And in her own words, she proclaimed, "Damn it, I'm going to have fun doing it!"

Question: I love this idea and I'm inspired to begin seeing *possibilities* **rather than roadblocks. But some of us have much more difficult challenges, and this reframing strategy just might not work out that easily. What about people who are dealing with more complex struggles?**

Very often our desire to *Be Amazing* is less goal-focused and comes from a deep, primal place of survival. For some of you, the next amazing quest for right now is about survival, and I want to share a story with you that will give you a sense of hope. I know in my heart that these survival stories are especially important, because they reveal the beauty and strength of the human spirit as it not only prevails but overcomes unimaginable struggles so that it may eventually *thrive*. These kinds of amazing stories remind me of a flower bulb that's been buried in the dark, damp, cold soil for the winter. We can't always see the progress unfolding underground as the roots take hold and the plant intuitively inches toward the warm sunlight to eventually break through the surface and bloom.

The amazing story I want to share with you starts off on a sad note, but there is a beautiful bloom at the end. I hope it resonates with you, and I hope it will also inspire you to hang in there and listen to what your heart calls you to do. Most of all, I hope it will inspire you to seek out the sunshine, too.

Jamie grew up in poverty with a severely abusive mother and was living alone. By the time she was thirteen, she was homeless. Her father died when she was very young, and her mother had simply left her on the streets. There certainly wasn't much around her that was amazing, and she certainly wasn't taught how to thrive and bloom; in fact, just the opposite. And as so often happens, we seek what we think we deserve, and when Jamie journeyed into adulthood, she ended up in a frightening and abusive marriage.

A few years ago, Jamie went through a horrible, fear-filled divorce after remaining in a marriage marked by domestic violence for about a decade. Suddenly, she found herself starting over as a single, middle-aged mother with young children and little else. Like that flower bulb, she started from below the ground craving the warmth and sunshine, but with no real reason to think that could ever possibly happen for her.

Throughout the marriage, she had been a stay-at-home mom, and her then-husband was extraordinarily controlling—a red flag often seen in domestic violence situations. She had no access to the family finances, and by the time the divorce and custody issues arose, all bank accounts were drained, the family vehicle was sold, and the house they had lived in (and believed they owned) had somehow ended up in her former husband's mother's name.

Jamie started over with quite literally nothing but the clothes she could fit into a suitcase and her most priceless treasures—her precious children. As Jamie shared her story with me, she said something incredibly important: "I know that the thoughts I had about my fears, my age, my low self-esteem, my lack of confidence, and my lack of work experience held me back. And ironically, these negative thoughts gave me hope, because I figured if I could begin to change my thoughts, I could begin to create a new life for me and my children."

I recently asked Jamie for an update on how she's doing now, and here's what she told me: "A lot has happened in my life between then and now; some unimaginable, and some miracles. I realized that my poverty mind-set was something I needed to work on every day. I also discovered that looking back for longer than a moment of reflection keeps me stuck in the past, and with it, the emotions and trauma of the past remain in the present." Learning to look to the future, with hope, with determination, and with awareness that she and her children deserve a wonderful, beautiful life, has truly changed her life. She called her transformation, now well underway, "difficult and extraordinary." I call it *amazing*.

Slowly but surely, hope-filled awareness begins to override the fears, and she is now determined to have a beautiful, extraordinary, maybe even amazing life that she can be proud of!

A few years ago, Jamie started a home-based social media business at her kitchen table. She found a client or two—including *Begin with Yes*—and has now begun to build a loyal base of customers who not only find her work amazing, but also her power to thrive despite unimaginable hardship astounding. Her clients include a publishing house, independent authors, and businesses with a social conscience. As she continues to pursue new business, she is committed to working with people who are making a difference.

Jamie agreed to share her story, not to make you feel sad or sympathetic, but to let you see how powerful our thoughts can be and how powerful rethinking "how we think" can be, too. More than anything, she wanted to encourage others to look forward, stay hopeful, and be focused on what could be. You have to remember that Jamie didn't wake up one day and suddenly have an amazing social media company. She started from scratch. She had to think about what she needed to learn and get specific about what kind of a company she wanted to have. And since she didn't have any real financial resources, her kitchen table was her office and the Internet her college degree. For me, reflecting on Jamie's journey often gets me off the couch and inspires me to take what I have and see what I can make happen. I hope it does the same for you.

Question: Jamie sounds pretty amazing, and your stories do help me understand the concepts you are sharing. These stories have helped me see what's possible for others and now I believe possible for me, too! I am ready. So, what's next?

To begin, please give yourself credit for being here and for reading these words. The truth is, your journey is well underway. For right now, I want you to begin to visualize "amazing." Imagine the amazing people, places, and things already part of your life. Remember something small but amazing that happened today. Find something near you right now that is amazing. How about something as simple as a light that comes on when you flip a switch? Or the bread you enjoyed at dinner. Isn't it amazing that you can mix a few ingredients together and then place it in a large box to bake?

We need to increase our own awareness of all the amazing things already in our lives, and together we are going to begin to focus our attention on seeing *amazing* wherever it appears. Maybe it's waking up and discovering that the sun is shining, or getting under a warm blanket on a cold winter's night. Look for *amazing* in your surroundings, in your blessings, in what you have, what you experience, what others are doing, and which dreams you've awakened. Look for *amazing* in big things and little things, too. It's the strangest thing, the more you look for miracles, the more miracles you discover! It's easier than you think, and being on the lookout for miracles and for *amazing* will shift things in your mind and in your heart. You will be realigned in ways that allow you to see the work differently, and your reality will begin to change. As your reality changes, your life will change, too. I am excited for what's around the corner for you and for me!

The other day, I got a note from a woman named Joan on my *Begin with Yes* Facebook page. She wrote: "I was putting gas in my car yesterday and noticed an elderly man at the pump in front of me. By the time I filled my tank, he had walked only as far as the back bumper of his car. I asked him if he needed help and he responded that he did. He gave me the money for the gas and asked if I could pump it for him. I told him I would and that he should go sit back in his car. He was so grateful and repeatedly thanked me, took my hand, and told me I had a good heart. This simple act of kindness made him happy and it made me feel good. I've been looking around when I'm out to see if I can help someone. Sometimes a situation presents itself, sometimes not. But when it does, it's amazing!" I want to thank Joan for reminding me of the profound beauty, simplicity, and power of *amazing* and how often that can become a shared experience with family, friends, coworkers, and strangers.

As you focus your attention, you too will begin to see how much good stuff is already happening around you, to you and through you, and your excitement about what's ahead will begin to expand in exciting, motivating ways.

I was sharing this story with my friend Eleanor, a successful professor and writer who has lived, and is living, an amazing life. As she reflected on this story, her eyes lit up and she said, "Those amazing moments are really what this is always about." She went on to explain how often we measure success with numbers and money and big accomplishments, but really all we actually have are our moments. The more amazing our moments, the more amazing our lives. Eleanor just finished writing an amazing book called *Counter Culture*. It's her memoir of growing up as one of twelve children and an attempt to document the lives of her family. I had the joy of watching Eleanor write her book, including all the stops and starts, the challenge of sorting out of what to tell and what could be left out, the complexities of having so much to share, and the life-altering realization that this was something she felt she was called, in a very powerful way, to complete.

The other day, Eleanor left a copy of her book at our house, and when I held it in my hand for the first time, I thought, "What an amazing accomplishment!" As I began to read, I fell in love with the amazing love story she had written. I am not sure if Eleanor ever said to herself, "I want to write an amazing book," but I am willing to bet that was her heart's desire. And guess what. She did it the only way possible—one step, or in Eleanor's case, one sentence—at a time!

I asked you to take this little detour with me, because I think it's important for us to notice how much magic is already in our world. As we notice all the amazingness around us, we are actually inviting more *amazing* to find us. This concept alone could be a book, and I hope you'll take this suggestion to heart. If you do that, then I will be comfortable getting back to your specific journey. Fair enough?

Assuming a resounding "Yes!" it's now time to get serious about your own amazingness and your own potential to eventually turn *Being Amazing* into an art form! It's now finally time to focus on the concrete steps that will get you moving toward your very own amazing destiny. I'd like to introduce you to the four basic steps we'll be taking together as we fire things up and move out of the thinking-about-it stage to the actually-making-it-happen phase. Are you ready to dive in?

Step One: Finding our "Spirit Blueprint"

This step requires us to get to know ourselves more intimately and invites us to take a closer look at the qualities that are uniquely ours. It is based upon my belief that we each have core passions that can become *touchstones* that awaken, guide, or lead us to discover a purpose (or purposes) that we are here to fulfill. I also believe that every purpose you uncover could easily have *amazing* attached to it. If we are called to do, or be, something, it's not rational to think that this something was meant to be anything other than amazing.

Some readers will already have definite ideas about their *spirit blueprint* and know where to begin, and others will need to spend a bit of time exploring this mystery. I would add here that sometimes what we think we know is really a doorway into a bigger, more exciting knowing, so please, even if you know what your passions are and even if you have already translated your passions into a purpose or goal, stay open to possible and natural new discoveries that might be waiting for you just around the corner.

If you are less clear, here are a few questions that, if you answer honestly, might give you some clues and at least get you thinking about where your life might soon be headed:

1. If there was nothing standing in your way, what would you be doing with your life?

2. When you were a kid, what did you want to be when you grew up?
3. What dreams did you pack away when life got complicated and the responsibilities of adulthood got in the way?
4. If you won the lottery, how would your life change? What would you want to do?
5. What gifts do you have that you are not finding time to pursue, much less share with the world?

Answering these questions will help you begin to rediscover your *spirit blueprint.* Allow yourself some time to think about these questions and enjoy the process of really listening to the answers. If you have family or friends, or even a therapist, you can explore some of these questions with the help of others. This process is really about reconnecting with who you are, and it's exciting and easier than you might think. Take your time and enjoy the discoveries you are making. And don't forget to write them down!

A friend of mine, Stacy, actually coined the phrase "spirit blueprint" as she was reviewing an early draft of this book. After talking, thinking, and writing about our passions and our purpose so much, the words were beginning to feel tired, and I wanted to add some energy to our conversation. "Spirit blueprint" became a new way of thinking and talking about these concepts. To some, this may even sound a bit "new-agey" at the moment, but give it a chance, because I think it will bring a unique viewpoint to the conversation.

If you're reading this book, I doubt that you are wondering why your spirit blueprint is important. But I want to remind you about something crucial: this book and my message are about *your* life. They're about taking what you have and making the most of it. They're not just about being the best you, they're about being the *real* you. Let that sink in. This is crucial and life-altering information. This journey you have embarked on is not just important, it's essential. It's not just a good thing to do, it actually has the potential to make the rest of your life the *best* of your life. What could be more important?

If you haven't already discovered how quickly time passes, you probably haven't lived long. If you haven't already discovered how life has a way of getting in the way of our dreams, you probably haven't dealt with the challenges most of us wake up to everyday. If you haven't almost forgotten some of your deepest and most passionate dreams, you probably haven't struggled with paying your bills, getting to work on time, having the demands on you seem so much greater than your energy or time allows.

If you're with me and this resonates with you, I need you to also hear that your time here is limited. You picked up this book because somewhere deep within, you know that you can refocus and you can use your time differently. You don't get to walk away from your responsibilities, and I certainly wouldn't want you to, but I *do* want you to have at least one thing from your *Be Amazing* list on your must-do list. If you don't have an amazing goal on your list, everything else will get in the way and your dreams will never see the light of day. You see, it's not really a question about why this is important; the real question is, what could be more important?

As we move forward, when I write about our spirit blueprint, I'm speaking to those things we feel drawn to, excited for, and curious about. We know we are close when we sense a deep desire and a psychic, emotional pull toward these thoughts, ideas, vocations, and avocations. We can't always explain why, but we sense that they are part of our DNA and just who we are.

And instead of writing about our "passions," I want to write about something more primal. When we uncover our spirit blueprint, we are reclaiming that soulful part of us that is calling us to move forward with a more authentic self. Again, this is not about our careers or businesses as much as it's about our lives. This may seem a little dramatic at the moment, but I hope it awakens in you a desire that has your name written all over it.

Eventually, you will understand that this entire process is not so much about finding our purpose as it is about a creating a life *with purpose*. This concept opens things up in extraordinary ways. Now we begin to see that we have very important things we are called to do. For the moment, we don't have to choose a specific goal, but rather focus on what we discover *in our core* that we are all about. Is it our love for science or is it a desire to be of service to others? Were we meant to perform or travel the world? Do we love being in nature or are we more alive in an urban area? Do we want to create or build something? I could go on and on, but you get the idea. This is our chance to welcome our spirit blueprint to reveal itself to us. This is our chance to rediscover what makes our hearts sing. Play with this and stay with this for a while. We don't have to work at finding our passions or really worry about what that will eventually reveal about our purpose(s). If we stay focused and engaged with our blueprint, our destiny or intended life has a way of finding us as we are, and *where* we are.

I want people to know that they can *Be Amazing* where they stand right now. Perhaps that means for the moment as a searcher or seeker of your spirit blueprint. This is a moment when I am going to ask you to stop reading and to stop thinking, too. I'd like you to do some freestyle writing about your feelings. I want to hear about your reconnection to those things that make you smile, get you excited, make you feel content, grounded, and yes, happy, too.

There's no need to judge, process, or stay within any lines; this is a time to just let yourself *go*. Maybe you feel like you're in your groove when you're baking, gardening, taking a road trip, or on a roller coaster. Maybe you feel most at home in a theater, meeting new people, or spending time with your best friends. Do you like camping, or shopping? Do you love dancing, drawing, researching solutions to a problem, working on your car, arranging flowers, or working out at the gym? What I hope you'll do right now is put down the book (or hit the pause button on your audiobook) and begin to write down all the beautiful thoughts and ideas floating through your heart and mind. There are no rules—just a blank canvas waiting for your crayons.

Once you're done, find a comfy chair to enjoy a cup of tea, or take your lovable pooch for a walk, stand up and stretch, or do some other relaxing, mindless activity and just breathe deeply for a bit. A few more thoughts might float into your mind, and, if that happens, jot them down if you can, but don't really do anything deep or demanding for a few minutes or even a few hours. Believe me, your journey toward amazing is well underway and you can get back to it soon enough!

Question: I enjoyed the break and also was surprised to see how many things ended up on my list. Could you explain what I should do next and how the list I have created will help me better understand my spirit blueprint?

First of all, thanks for being open to this discovery process. What you've done is actually spent some time looking at that unique and personal blueprint that belongs to you alone, and you've given your heart an opportunity to speak freely and openly without worrying about being practical or sensible.

The next step is to look at what's in your heart—in this case, the list you've created with your *mind*. It's time to process what you've discovered, and that's something you can do alone or with a friend or even a group of friends. Your mission is to translate what your heart shared into actual amazing possibilities that you can begin to move from the "possible" column to the "actual" column. In other words, you soon will have a list of actual, very specific opportunities that have been identified that you can choose to *Be Amazing*.

As we move forward, you will be using a simple four-step process that will get you moving and keep you moving in the direction of *amazing*. My wish for you is that after a little practice, this will become less of a process and more about just how you operate. Remember when you first learned to ride a bike? Think of this next phase as the training wheels phase of learning something new. Once you get the hang of it, you'll be able to take off those training wheels and head off in all kinds of directions and on to all kinds of adventures.

Now, alone or with a few trusted friends, it's time to pull out that list you created and discover how the things that make you excited or smile all offer glimpses into the things you are here to do. Again, remember that it's quite possible that you will discover more than one area you will want to explore and move forward with. Soon, I will ask you to choose one area to practice. Later, you will be free to multitask and explore *Being Amazing* in whatever areas you feel drawn to.

Let me give you a few examples of how to translate your spirit blueprint into one of your purposes. If you love spending time with your grandchildren, then maybe you could consider being an amazing grandparent. If you love spending time outdoors, maybe you could begin to explore careers that would put you outdoors rather than a job that would have you at a desk from 9 to 5. If your favorite high school or college course was biology, which careers might resonate with you? (And don't worry if you didn't love biology; that just means your purpose probably isn't to be a biology teacher.)

What you need to do is take all that you discovered or, rather, *uncovered* about your heart's desire and translate that into goals. Some people feel overwhelmed at this juncture because there are so many paths or directions they want to pursue. If that's how you're feeling, remember that the quest to *Be Amazing* is not a one-time or even one-way trip, and, as your life unfolds, you will have all kinds of opportunities to pursue amazingness.

Before we move onto your next question, I want to check in with you about something really important as we move forward. I hope you're excited and hopeful, but I want to also remind you to relax into this and be calm. We are not fighting a battle here, we are learning new skills and new ways of looking at things.

I don't want to slow you down at all, but I do want you to be as nonjudgmental as you can be and to not try to rush or force answers to questions that don't really have to be answered right now! I have found in my own life that as long as I am keeping my mind and heart open and as long as I keep taking small steps toward goals of any size, I am discovering what I need as I need it. So, keep at it but *relax* a bit, too! And now, if *you're* ready, *I'm* ready for the next question!

Question: And I'm ready, too. What should I do next?

Step Two: Making a Decision

It's now time to declare where you'll be headed so you can begin the first trip that you are destined to take! This step simply requires us to make a decision and a commitment so that we can move from the "understanding what our blueprint is calling us to do" phase to the "making it my reality" phase.

This is where you will decide that you want to be an amazing restaurateur, nurse, baker, or candlestick maker. This is where you will decide to go after finding what's been hidden in your heart and learning how to unpack it. And of course, it's quite likely your blueprint will lead to more than one goal. But as we begin, you will want to choose one exciting target to focus on to get you started. What have you discovered? What are you called to do? Here are some examples:

- I am called to be an artist and photograph images from nature.
- I am called to be dancer.
- I am called to be a minister helping others deal with the life challenges we all face.
- I am called to parent or grandparent.
- I am called to be an entrepreneur and buy old run-down houses and then breathe a new and beautiful life into them.
- I am called to bake delicious cakes and pastries.
- I am called to travel and make the strangers I meet my friends.

- I am called to be a teacher, a Broadway actor, a yoga instructor.
- I am called to invent things.
- I am called to be a magician, a speech pathologist, a small business owner, a journalist, or a florist.

Now add a personal goal or two to this list and then add the word "amazing" in front of each goal. Look what happens:

- I am called to be an amazing photographer capturing images from nature.
- I am called to be an amazing dancer.
- I am called to be an amazing minister looking out for the needs of others.
- I am called to be an amazing parent or grandparent.
- I am called to be an amazing entrepreneur, buy old rundown houses, and then breathe a new and beautiful life into them.
- I am called to be an amazing baker creating delicious cakes and pastries.
- I am called to be an amazing seeker and travel and make the strangers I meet my friends.
- I am called to be an amazing teacher, a Broadway actor, a yoga instructor.
- I am called to be an amazing inventor.
- I am called to be an amazing magician, speech pathologist, small business owner, journalist, or florist.

Something very important has been set in motion, because our goals are now not simply about making something happen, but about making something *amazing* happen. We are becoming amazing magicians, amazing bankers, amazing dog walkers, amazing granddaughters and daughters-in-law, amazing neighbors, amazing inventors, amazing dancers, amazing writers and bakers, and on and on! There's a whole lot of amazingness possible, and my goal is to help you get there while having as much fun as possible.

During this process, you may discover that you are already fully or partially engaged in your goal. You may have found your way in the direction of your heart's desire and now will just need to become more focused as you take it to the next level. Or you may have discovered that you are called toward a brand-new pathway. Whichever way you have discovered, wonderful opportunities to be more fully realized and engaged in an amazing life are around the corner.

Again, I would not be surprised to hear that you have many goals or areas in which you'd like to *Be Amazing*, but for now, it's important to choose one goal to focus on. Think of this as a skill-building process. Once you experience how to *Be Amazing* in one arena, you will have the opportunity to *Be Amazing* in as many ways as you want. Right now, being focused will help you be successful. I wouldn't encourage anyone to learn three new foreign languages at once but rather would encourage you to master one and then move onto the next one, and that's basically what I hope you'll do right now! One goal at a time and, as you will soon discover, one step at a time, too.

Question: Thanks for the reminder to relax. I will take a couple of deep breaths and relax as best as I can before moving forward with this! I am just so ready to begin *Being Amazing* **at something, so the obvious question is, where do I start?**

You keep making me smile, and I am excited for you as we move forward. Let me begin by pointing out that you have already shown signs of being an amazing student! And you must know that your adventure is well underway. You don't have to wait to begin, because you actually began when you picked up this book and held it in your hands!

Question: As I begin to see my potential for *Being Amazing*, I have to ask myself: why, in the past, have so many of us have settled for less?

I believe we have settled for less because we were mistakenly told some version of "Don't get too big for your britches." This well-intended parental message may have been an attempt to keep us humble, but it had the unintended consequence of teaching us not to shine and not to reach for the stars. In essence, we were taught *not* to *Be Amazing*.

Here's what I wish parents would teach their children and what you can now relearn for yourself: You can *Be Amazing* and humble at the same time. You can *Be Amazing* and help others *Be Amazing*, too. *Being Amazing* doesn't diminish anyone around you or make you better than anyone else; it makes you *you*. Please don't think it's arrogant to *Be Amazing*; it's actually arrogant not to boldly own and express the passions and gifts you've been given to share with the universe.

So, if you're ready to choose your "*Be Amazing* test project," I am excited to hear it. Remember, the world is your oyster, but there's nothing wrong with starting small. And there's nothing wrong with starting big, either. And no matter where you begin, your *Be Amazing* journey is now officially well underway! You're now ready for step three.

Step Three: Discover What Amazing Will Look Like

This step requires you to identify what the specific attributes of *Being Amazing* are for the goal you have chosen. This is where you will be describing in words what you will be creating in action. This is your chance to envision how whatever it is you want will actually look like when you get there. You can begin this process by yourself, and then you may want to share your thoughts with other people who are on their own amazing journey. This sharing will help you learn to articulate what you see in your own mind's eye and allow your very unique and very personal vision to be enhanced by the ideas that others may be willing to share with you. This is a fun and reflective process where you add some details to what an amazing artist, real estate agent, parent, social worker, baker, or restaurant owner would look like.

Here are a few of my ideas about what a specific amazing would look like:

An amazing photographer might be passionate about the images she captures. She would have a decent camera or even iPhone, would have studied Photoshop and Lightroom, would have a knowledge of composition and a developed eye for the beauty around her.

An amazing baker would have a teacher or mentor that knows baking secrets, would practice baking and getting feedback from others, would get to know other extraordinary bakers and learn from them.

An amazing teacher would have a skill to share, would love working with others, would be excited and passionate about what she was teaching.

An amazing neighbor would go the extra mile in helping to get your mail when you're away on vacation or lend you that cup of sugar or another ingredient when you realize you're falling short during a recipe.

If you chose (as I did) to be an amazing grandparent, your job now is to describe what being an amazing grandparent looks like. In other words, what does an amazing grandparent look like to you? Does he or she listen and stay involved with their grandchildren? Does she call or meet up or Facetime on a regular basis? Does he remember birthdays and other special holidays? Does she help with Halloween costumes, teach how to tie shoes, or bake chocolate chip cookies? Do amazing grandparents go to school plays, read bedtime stories in person, on audio files or tapes, or live-chat through Facetime? Does an amazing grandparent carry special treats in his coat pockets?

You can even ask your children and your grandchildren what an amazing grandfather or grandmother would look like to them. This discovery process is very personal, and you can look around for role models, but try to keep this real and relevant to you and your own life. I am quite certain that your idea of being an amazing grandparent might be different from mine, but that is part of what makes this journey so special. *You* get to decide what amazing looks like, and then you begin to turn these attributes into becoming a real and amazing grandparent. Soon you will get to go from the theoretical, thinking about it step by step, to the *joyful*, making it become reality.

It's also important to remember that your amazing isn't about being perfect or better than someone else; it's about being as good and as much as you want to be. And we always get to adjust where we are heading, and what amazing looks like. We learn as we go along, and always remind yourself that amazing is not a destination, but, truly, an approach to achieving your goals, honoring your heart's desires, and creating a life that has meaning to you.

I offer the suggestions above just to give you a starting place. Again, your idea of what an amazing baker looks like could be quite different from mine. And after all, this is about *your* dream, and so your vision of amazing will drive the process. So be sure that you take the time to really think about what amazing would look like for you. Not only is that important, it's absolutely essential!

Let me tell you the story of a colleague and friend of mine who has figured out what going that extra mile is all about, and who understands how powerful it can be. Teresa will be surprised to see her story here, because she probably doesn't realize just how amazing she is.

Teresa is a working mom who takes care of two teenagers and also helps care for her elderly mother. Like most of us, she has her fair share of self-doubt, a to-do list a mile long, a demanding job, and limited time, and these would each be a good enough excuse for taking a pass at stepping into her full potential. But that's not the Teresa I've gotten to know.

I first met Teresa when she was recommended as a potential public relations consultant to work with our company. She and her boss, Matt, came in for a preliminary conversation with me and a few members of our senior team, and we knew within minutes that this new professional relationship would be a "go."

Now, I've worked with many PR folks over the years—most of them good, a few even very good—but Teresa had something extra that set her apart and made her amazing. First of all, she listened. She didn't pretend to be paying attention; she was actually tuning in to what we needed to share. She was warm, outgoing, and enthusiastic—even excited. We felt this was someone who already liked us and our company and someone who wanted to be part of our team.

She smiled and laughed easily and seemed genuinely interested in our concerns, and we felt understood and heard, which instilled a sense in us that Teresa could really help us and be an asset to our company.

Before our initial conversation, she had googled our company and visited our website, so she already knew our mission and had a good sense of who we were and what we were about. Again, this felt like we were talking with someone who really cared and wanted to work with us!

Once Teresa started working with us, we knew that our intuition was on the money. She spent time in our headquarters, she introduced herself to employees and clients, and she gave us ideas about what we could do better. But she wasn't just an *idea* person; she was a roll-up-your-sleeves-and-let-me-help-you-do-it person! And in the category "small things count big," the other day Teresa was picking me up for a lunch meeting and I noticed she had tuned the Sirius radio channel to my favorite Broadway station. Kind of amazing, huh?

I wanted to share Teresa's story, because it demonstrates how going a bit beyond where most go in terms of customer service and relationship and community building can make a huge difference. Her enthusiasm helps. Her warm smile and contagious laugh helps. Her "can-do" attitude helps. And her love for what she is doing makes it clear that she is focusing her energy on work that she loves, and that makes working with her an amazing experience for folks lucky enough to be alongside her.

Question: I have made my decision and now know what *Being Amazing* **is going to look like for me. I am cautiously excited and ready to actually roll up my sleeves and get moving. Maybe it's nervous energy or excitement, but whatever it is, I am ready to hear more about the next step. In other words, I want to actually get my hands on that clay and see what I can make happen!**

I am as excited as you are, so let's dig in.

Step Four: Making It Happen

This will be the time you actually take that mound of clay, or the pen and ink, or the flour and eggs, and begin to create your very own amazing masterpiece!

I am willing to bet that you already see where we're headed. Step four is where we begin taking those small steps toward our big goals. During this phase of our adventure, we will explore the seemingly small action steps that bridge the gap between *ordinary* and *amazing*.

More precisely, this is when we'll begin taking small steps towards being amazing by focusing on those specific characteristics you described a short time ago. I'll explain why small action steps are essential, and how they work. And we'll also learn why they are so effective and how they get us through all kinds of roadblocks, upsets, and challenges.

For example, if you noted that having a favorite candy bar in your pocket is a part of being an amazing grandfather, then that's a really easy step to take! Get that candy bar in your pocket. You may want to figure out how to have more face time with your grandchildren. You may realize that if you don't schedule and commit, time will slip away and the positive actions you have intended will instead end up as good intentions you've fallen short on. So, get a time scheduled.

If being an amazing nurse means getting more education in an area you want to specialize in, you will need to begin to chart out how you will make that happen. Small steps might include talking to a coworker who already has that expertise or exploring continuing ed opportunities nearby. You might meet with your HR department or your supervisor to uncover time-off possibilities and financial assistance to take advantage of important training opportunities.

Let me tell you about a friend of mine, Brian Hutchison. Brian is a professional actor based in New York City, and though most of his professional career has found him sharing his passion with audiences in the theater, he's also graced numerous movie and television screens. Now, Brian's a very modest guy, but when I asked him recently what he thought the qualities are that makes someone an amazing actor, his reply was very honest and heartfelt. He said, "Being an amazing actor takes talent and hard work, but probably most of all, *tenacity*. I created an idea of what I could be capable of *in my mind's eye* when I was just starting out. I was very shy when I was younger, and speaking in front of groups wasn't something that came easy. Learning to 'become' another person, and learning lines, allowed me to experience *having a voice* for the very first time. I think goal setting is incredibly important. And don't be afraid to be *fearless*."

The last time I saw Brian in person, he was on top of the world, starring in the Broadway hit *The Boys in the Band*. It brings me great joy to see him so happy and successful in his ever-evolving journey. And I look forward to what he may do next.

OK, time for another brief pause. We have covered a lot of material, and you have some real work (and play!) ahead of you. Let's stop thinking and just *be* for a minute.

Inhale. Exhale.

And again.

Now take a walk, empty the dishwasher, call a neighbor, or balance your checking account. I will be here when you're ready.

Welcome back! I think the next section will cover many of the questions you still have and will help you better understand and actualize these four steps.

Question: That's great to hear, because I know it would help if you could talk about some of the challenges I might expect. In other words, what's going to get in my way, and what can I do to work around the challenges that I am pretty sure may pop up?

Another great question and one not everyone would have asked, so good for you! This is a great time to remind you of the power of your thoughts. We spent a lot of time talking about how clever we are at making up realities that hold us back. And as we dive deeper into some of our challenges, please keep your power and creativity front and center. So, with that, let's look at some of the potential twists and turns ahead, and especially some of the so-called roadblocks, necessary detours, and typical resistance you are about to discover. And then more important, let's talk about some of the work-arounds or tools you can use to stay on track and keep moving forward. Here are some of the questions that are most often asked about dealing with the challenges that may be part of our journey.

Question: What do I do when I am feeling stuck, and how do I keep moving forward?

First of all, don't let that *feeling-stuck* feeling throw you. I'd be surprised if anyone reading this hasn't felt stuck, and not overreacting is key. In fact, invite the feeling in. Feeling stuck is part of the game; it's to be expected and doesn't need to slow us down for long. The first thing you might try when you're feeling stuck is to simply shift your attention to another goal related to your *Be Amazing* journey. For example, if you're working at being an amazing writer and you find yourself staring at the keyboard and the blank screen, instead of writing, try doing some research on the subject you're writing about. Or, if you are trying to be an amazing gardener and it's snowing outside, go to the library or google new gardening blogs that can increase your knowledge base and inspire you while you are waiting for spring!

This shifting of emphasis not only keeps you goal-focused, but focused on an aspect of the goal you can feel some positive energy around. If you're feeling stuck, ask yourself, "What's another area of this goal I can shift my attention to?" Your answer will keep you moving, and you will soon find yourself returning to that stuck point and moving forward there.

If this doesn't seem to help, try shifting your attention to something else on your to-do list. Clean out that junk drawer, go grocery shopping, or clean up your address list. This shift will keep you productive and actually energize you.

Another option is to do something physical like go for a walk, turn on some music and dance, play with you pooch or your kids, or make some cookies. You can't be moving and stuck at the same time, so keep moving! I am not trying to just keep you busy; I'm trying to teach you to not turn that being-stuck feeling to a staying-stuck reality. One other idea you may find helpful: stop telling yourself you're stuck! Sure, you can indulge the thought for a moment, but then reframe it to "I'm having trouble writing right now, so I'm going to do some research and I'm continuing my quest." Pay attention to what you're telling yourself, because you are not just talking, you're taking it in, too.

If you find "being stuck" is a chronic problem, you may have some work to do in this area. Sometimes feeling stuck is really a sign that we are scared or angry, and sometimes it's a sign that we are focusing on something that doesn't come from our heart and soul. So be sure and check in about where you are stuck and see what that my reveal. One of my favorite bumper stickers is "What do we know that we are not letting ourselves see?" Ask yourself that question often and smile every time you uncover something helpful. Then, of course, do something about what you learned!

Question: How do I deal with lack of financial and other resources?

This is a time to focus more on what you *have* rather than on what you *don't have*. If you want to dress with amazing style, you may have to shop in consignments shops. Better yet, you may want to get a part-time job in a shop, so you can get first dibs on new arrivals. Making a list of what you have to work with is a great starting place to then identify what you need. And it's important to get real and get specific about what you need. Without a "real" number, it's difficult to establish a goal to reach. If you need to find tuition money, you can start by scheduling an appointment with a financial advisor at a nearby college.

I also think that we use our lack of resources as a reason not to pursue a goal or dream. So, we need to take it one step at a time. Ask yourself, "What steps I can take while I explore finding resources?" For example, needing money for college doesn't stand in your way of making an appointment to tour the campus. I find that once we begin to take the steps that we can take, the next steps seem to become clearer and much more obvious. Doing what you *can* is a great way to discover ways of finding what you *need*. The best way to discover financial aid opportunities for tuition is by speaking to someone who understands that world better than you.

Also, look for work-arounds and get your friends to help you think of ways to get what you need. Could you work part-time in an art supply store to earn extra money and a store discount to buy art supplies? Could you walk a friend's dog while you walk your dog to earn money to take tap dance lessons? Or would your dance instructor trade dance lessons for child care?

State your resource challenge and then come up with partial or even complete solutions. Keep taking small steps while waiting for the bigger pieces to fall into place. Do what you can with what you have and stay open to unusual solutions that are just waiting to be discovered along the way. Lack of resources is a very real problem, and you may have to be creative about solving it.

It's important to remember that many of our amazing dreams take *time*, and some can take much longer than others. Jan is a Facebook friend of mine who has had her heart set on moving to Puerto Rico for some time now so she can help with the ongoing efforts regarding hurricane recovery. She has more than a few things slowing her down and a few important family things that are close to her heart that must be considered before she can commit to any plans. She knows it will take a while to get there, but she refuses to give up! Not long ago, I was vacationing in Puerto Ricco and received her note, "Buenas Dias, Paul! Are you in Puerto Rico? If you are, would you write my name on a pebble and toss it into the ocean? Because one day I shall walk the beaches there!"

She went on to mention that she is in constant contact with two local volunteer coordinators and has also made a connection with a woman who has relocated to Puerto Rico, helping to blaze the trail for her! She has even gone on to apply for a full-time position with a disaster relief organization.

Jan is anxiously awaiting the arrival of her third grandchild in a few months, so her life will be getting a bit busier; but her thoughts and wishes are still right on track, and she is planning a trip to Puerto Rico this year. In her own poignant words, "I have not given up on *me*."

I love Jan's story, and her dream that she fully visualizes. I know one day she will walk on that beach and help the amazing people of Puerto Rico continue to rebuild their beautiful island. And one of the last things I did before returning home to the States was to write Jan's name on a small stone and toss it into the ocean, as she had asked.

Question: How to I keep moving forward despite lack of family or network support?

Having the support of family and friends is a wonderful gift, but it's not a guarantee. If it's not happening, the first thing to do is be sure you have asked for the support. Often, we are so caught up in our own work and quests that we haven't filled in those around us. Explaining what you're doing and why it's important may go a long way. I have people say to me, "Why didn't you explain what you wanted? I want to help and support, I just didn't know what you were up to and didn't know what you wanted or needed from me." So, if you're feeling that no one cares, that's the first thing to check.

The second thing to try is another focus shift. Identify two or three people in your life whom you'd like to be on your team and figure out what their goals are and volunteer to be on their team. Being focused is so important, but being entirely self-focused is a mistake, as we risk becoming isolated, self-centered, and, at the extreme, narcissistic. Paying attention to someone else's dream is good for us, good for them, and just plain good *karma*.

Finally, if you're still not getting the encouragement from folks in your circle, it's time to widen the circle a bit and bring some new minds and hearts into your life. And the best way to do that is to look for opportunities to support others. My dear friend Mark taught me a long time ago that when you change someone's life, you change your own. And when you get that something as simple as a smile or a few kind words can change a day and even a life, you will make that a natural part of your daily mission, and one day soon you will discover there are some new people in your life!

If you find yourself more and more frustrated or angry with the people around you, that might not be your fault, but it *is* your issue. And it's your issue because you simply can't change everyone around you, and you're going to have to figure out how best to deal with them. And it's your issue because it suggests that you have a bit of inner work to do. Accept the fact that you have difficult people in your life and then also acknowledge that it's not your job to fix or change them. It's your job to move forward without their support or help or encouragement. Once you focus on what you need to do rather than how you're going to fix other people, you will have experienced a life-changing insight!

Question: Do you have any advice about people with physical challenges or illnesses?

Let me tell you a story about someone I met at an annual meeting at my organization a few years ago named Randy Pierce. When he was just twenty-two years old, Randy unexpectedly lost his vision over the course of two short weeks due to a devastating neurological disease. When he turned thirty-nine, the same episodic illness returned in full force, confining him to a wheelchair. Over the next two years, Randy worked tirelessly to regain his strength to become the first blind hiker to summit all of New Hampshire's forty-eight 4,000-foot mountains, run two Boston Marathons, compete in multiple "Tough Mudder" obstacle courses, and climb Mt. Kilimanjaro with the help of his team of ten friends and his guide dog, Mighty Quinn, by his side.

My guess is that Randy understood *amazing* before he became blind, but what's unique about his story is that he didn't let a major setback *set him back* for long. Today, Randy is a very busy keynote speaker, author, and blind mountain climber and adventurer who travels nationally inspiring all within earshot. You can read more of his story in his book, *See you at the Summit*.

Another remarkable man who has inspired me tremendously is David. David is a gentleman in his fifties who was born with Down syndrome. He lives with his older brother Tom, who has cared for David since 2009 when he took over guardianship when both of their parents passed away. Three times a week, David reports faithfully to the supermarket in his hometown, where he's worked for the last twenty-five years. On any given day as you're absently roaming the grocery store aisles or doing the mad dash to pluck a few last-minute items off the shelf, your life is made much easier by people like David. He's employed as a blocker, an all-important supermarket function that keeps order among the endless myriad of cans, jars, boxes, and other ribbons of color that line the shelves. David ensures their labels are turned front and center and pulled forward to the edge for the ease of customers. David brings so many gifts to everyone he meets, and he takes incredible pride in his job every single day he's there. He has rarely missed a day of work in his two decades of employment, and his brother Tom says, "He has such great concentration that when he's finished in an aisle, it looks just like a painting; it's so perfect!"

David's boss, Carl, the regional store manager, couldn't agree more. "Employing David is simply a tremendous 'win' for us," he said. "His work ethic is top-notch, and we couldn't imagine our team existing without him. He's the 'icing on the cake' for us."

What David brings to his job every single day is a level of *amazing* that can inspire us all. His coworkers and his customers alike consider David an integral part of their "family." He goes about his day quietly, and without fanfare, and spreads joy to all in his path.

Question: Could you give me some ideas that will keep me moving forward, even when I'm feeling overwhelmed?

Great question, as usual. The key word here is "feeling." Feeling overwhelmed is a pretty universal experience, but we need to remember that it's more often a feeling than a reality. And the reason for the feeling, more often than not, is simply that we are allowing our imagination to run wild and letting way too much information in all at once. There are two things we can do when we're feeling overwhelmed: the first is to focus on the one most immediate thing that needs attention and take care of that. And the second thing we can do is ask for help.

This story demonstrates these two actions beautifully. It begins at Alexander's Guest House in Key West, Florida. My partner, Mike, and I have been fortunate to stay there more than once over the years, and whenever we visit my kids and grandkids (who all live in Florida), we begin thinking of ways we might turn that family time into a chance to visit Key West again. When we are lucky enough to make that happen, we always go back to Alexander's for a few very important reasons.

First of all, the place is beautiful, with picturesque, lush grounds. The beds are comfortable, and the breakfast is not just healthy (which Mike likes), but also delicious (which, as you already know, I tend to celebrate!). There are lots of beautiful places to stay in Key West with comfortable beds and good food. But the reason we always head back to our favorite spot is that it feels like we are returning home for a visit with an extended family who are just as excited to see us as we are to see them.

The manager, Laura, who has her own amazing story to tell, has created a family-like environment that is welcoming and inclusive in some incredible ways. She and the owners had decided that Alexander's was going to be a place where guests felt like *family*, not just because they were treated like family (in the nicest possible way), but because that's how they actually felt about us. And you can be sure that as nice as I think Mike and I are, we aren't any more special than anyone else who stays there. But, they make us *feel* as if we were.

Now, fast-forward to Hurricane Irma of 2017, which battered the Florida Keys, caused a mass exodus, left behind mass destruction on parts of the island, and crippled the very important tourist industry throughout the entire area. Many of those in the Alexander's extended family stayed in touch during and after the hurricane, and Laura did her best to keep us all informed. Once it was safe for the guesthouse staff to return home, they discovered minor damage, some significant personal losses, and the realization that many customers cancelled their future reservations. Having no guests meant no income, and that meant no money for payroll at a time when their employees were most vulnerable. It was all overwhelming.

But here's where things get even more interesting, and more amazing! The owners of Alexander's decided, even though they weren't quite sure *how* they would do it, to continue paying their staff as they all got back on their feet. They put all the things that needed attention aside for a moment and focused on *the one thing* they could do. Laura reached out to their community of "family" and described what was going on. Almost immediately, some guests who had room reservations booked for the future offered to prepay for their stay, to help with cash flow. Then new reservations began to come in as a show of solidarity and support. A *GoFundMe* account was established to help staff put their lives and homes back together, and soon it felt like the storm had not only passed, but the sun was coming out! Putting all their efforts into just one solitary need created a space for other things to get done, in a sequential way. One of my favorite questions to ask is "Now what?" When I am feeling overwhelmed, I use the question to help me sort through all the thoughts swirling around in my head and then choose something concrete I can focus on *right now.*

Now fast-forward again to a letter the Alexander's family just received:

Hello Dear Guests,

Thank you . . . so very much to all of you who reached out to us at Alexander's to offer your help.

When I sent out the email at the end of our work day to share where we were at with our dear guest house, we returned in the morning to find 145 emails and 40 phone messages from so many of you offering to pay towards your balances to help keep us afloat and also wanting to make donations to the staff. Robyn and I, who opened that morning, stood quietly humbled and in awe.

Our eyes filled with tears of pure joy and gratitude. We were completely taken aback at how generous and willing you were to reach out and help us. . . . This message is to ALL of YOU (and you know who you are our little angels) . . . saying a HUGE THANK YOU! We all are so incredibly grateful to you . . . for your calls sending good wishes, your concern, your love, support, loyalty and humanity during this very difficult, crazy, uncertain time.

Thank you also for your donations to the Hurricane IRMA staff relief fund as well. We plan on taking 10% off the top and paying it forward, donating that 10% to an organization the Alexander's staff will decide together on.

We will also assess within our staff what each needs (home/car issue or has a partner who is not working and needs the financial assistance), but mainly it will just be split equally among all staff members once the largest issues are taken care for each staff member. Each staff member plans on paying it forward to help others as well.

I have felt overwhelmed, not knowing where to begin when it seems everywhere I look, someone truly needs help. Someone close to me recently told me, "This is not a sprint; it is a marathon . . . pace yourself." I realized how correct they were. I needed to just pick a starting point and work from there. So, I began right here at home and will continue to extend as far as I can.

I am proud to say that everyone here at Alexander's has this same commitment. Wonderful guests like you and a wonderful Alexander's team has created quite a magical community that we are honored to be a part of.

Alexander's is up and running and waiting for your next visit, so we can give you the biggest, squishiest hug ever!

Thank you for being a part of our lives and letting us be a part of yours.

With love and gratitude,
Laura and All of Your Family at Alexander's Guesthouse

You may be touched by this letter; I know I was. And I knew I wanted to share this story with all of you so that you could see how feeling overwhelmed doesn't have to stop you. And not surprisingly, this story gave me an excuse to remind you how *amazing* happens and how much wonderful, powerful, and positive energy is set in motion when we embrace the challenges we face. I also wanted to use this story because it gives me the opportunity to share again how important little gestures can be. A few come to mind, including:

- remembering guests by their first name
- hiring staff who love people
- taping a handwritten welcome note on a returning guest's room doors, and
- baking cookies and leaving them on the kitchen counter for guests to enjoy.

Question: How do I move past fear and depression?

You could be writing this book, because you are asking all the right questions and making it easy for me! Let's start with *fear*. It's a feeling that is usually signaling *danger ahead*. But it's also a feeling that pops up when we are trying something new, stepping out of our comfort zone, or taking risks to pursue a better life. What has worked for me and so many others I have worked with is to stop trying to stop the fear and learn that you can do something even when you're scared. Senator John McCain famously said, "Courage is not the absence of fear, but the capacity to act despite our fears." This concept of courage is incredibly powerful, and we just need to practice doing this to prove to ourselves that it's true. I still think it's a good idea to look both ways before crossing the street, but if there are no cars coming or the sign says walk, keep moving!

When it comes to depression or other mental health issues, I urge you to get help. The stigma of mental health problems will soon be a thing of the past, but right now, there are folks around you who might not have evolved as much we would have liked. You don't need someone to urge you to seek medical attention when you have strep throat or migraine headaches, and you shouldn't hesitate to seek help when you are experiencing depression or other mental health issues. If whatever is going on is slowing you down, then the very first thing on your to-do list is to get some help. It can be one of the most powerful gifts you give yourself.

Question: Any suggestions on working through low self-esteem, and the lack of confidence?

The first thing I'd say here is you're in great company. Most of us have struggled with, or still struggle with, self-esteem. And if I had to choose between an inflated and unearned high regard for myself or self-esteem issues, I'd choose the self-esteem issues. It's a healthy place to start. The biggest mistake people make in this area is to think that they need to deal with low self-esteem before they begin, when just the opposite is true. Begin, and your self-esteem almost always begins to grow. If you expect and accept that self-esteem issues will sometimes get in your way and you move forward anyway, you will discover how powerful you really are. Doing things even when you aren't feeling up to it is a great confidence-builder.

Question: What if I am just too tired to take even the smallest of steps?

If you're feeling too tired to take that small step, this is the time to break down your small step into an even *smaller* step—the one you can manage before getting into bed. If writing even a paragraph of your unfinished memoir is too much, try writing a sentence. If composing a Facebook post is overwhelming, take a photo of the cat so you can use it tomorrow morning when you have more energy. The point is not to march to the point of exhaustion, but rather to take one small step toward your dream before heading to bed.

I've also found that often when we are too tired, it's because we have not been engaged. Try shifting your energy toward something you love or feel passion around, and you may discover you have an unexpected and sudden burst of energy.

Finding our passion or purpose is often a subtle, growing awareness of what makes you happy or excited, and learning to take small steps in that direction. Dort Rothafelm is a consultant who helps get new restaurants off the ground. On any given day, he interviews and mentors a wide variety of people, and he believes strongly that finding one's passion in life makes all the difference. He explains, "If a person doesn't have an activity that truly *excites* them outside of their profession, they cannot be genuinely passionate about their performance. One of the questions I ask of every applicant I interview is 'What are you *passionate* about in your personal life? What makes you spring out of bed with excitement knowing you get to do that *one thing*?' If the candidate cannot convey their passion to me, they have a very slim chance of getting hired. I see no point in serving without passion." Sometimes our passions will line up with how we earn a living, and other times we get to nurture our passions outside of our daily jobs. The story I told about starting a community theater certainly falls into that category, and even my writing career has evolved alongside of my other wonderful job of running a not-for-profit. I once coached an attorney with three kids who wanted to be a poet instead of a lawyer. As we talked, I encouraged him to be bold and have one foot midair but also reminded him to keep one foot grounded in reality. We finally agreed that he could be a lawyer to support his family and be a poet to support his dream! It may be true that we can't have it all, but it's also true that we can have more than what we've been taught! And for many of us, as we pursue our passions, we discover ways to incorporate them into our work—or our passions actually evolve into our jobs.

We need to begin gently moving into the places we just naturally feel pulled and drawn to. Tonight, as you fall asleep, think about what truly brings you joy. What is it that will make you want to whip off your covers in anticipation of what you get to do tomorrow?

Question: What if I fall short or just plain fall down? How do I keep moving?

Well, if we're being completely truthful here, one thing you can certainly bet on is falling short from time to time. That's what makes us human! The twist is that we often see this as a negative, while it's really just completely natural. The second part of your question is really the question at hand, and I do have some suggestions that will help.

Here's another story I love to tell, not only because it illustrates "amazing" in action, but also because it speaks to the ups and downs we all experience.

Do you remember the Stephen King book *Carrie* about the teenage girl with telekinetic powers? She lived with her mother, who was an over-the-top character who struggled with mental illness that was marked by outrageous religious beliefs and convictions. Carrie was emotionally repressed and tormented by her mother, and to make matters worse, she was bullied and terribly mistreated by her classmates. Ultimately, she reached her breaking point and in an act of rage used her telekinetic powers to destroy her high school and, ultimately, her entire town.

Well, Stephen King's scary book became a pretty scary movie and then, about forty years ago, became a Broadway musical, which unfortunately turned into one of the biggest Broadway flops of all time. This flop was so big, it became legendary! It was even featured on the cover of a book devoted to Broadway flops titled, *Not Since Carrie*.

You have to wonder to yourself, "Who would read Stephen King's novel, or watch the movie, and think, 'Gee, this would make a great musical!'" Well, on opening night, the audience couldn't stop laughing. Apparently, what was scary as a book and a movie had seemingly evolved into a musical that was anything but scary!

The actress Betty Buckley, whom you may remember as the stepmother on the television show *Eight Is Enough*, played Carrie's mother, and the play ends with the mother and daughter actually killing each other. They both fall to the floor dead, and then the stage and theater goes totally black. In the darkness, the audience—who had been laughing throughout the performance—now began booing. The young actress playing Carrie, still on the floor in the dark, was shaken and scared and whispered to Betty, "What do we do?"

And Betty whispered back, "We stand up."

And as they stood, the stage lights came up completely, and the entire audience jumped to its feet for a full house standing ovation. I actually asked Betty about this story, and she verified it was absolutely true, saying she didn't know if the audience was cheering their performance or their courage for getting up. But either way, it was an amazing moment!

Betty went on to say, "It was the most enthusiastic audience response of my entire career." Given the reviews that followed, I know, and I think Betty knew, there wouldn't have been a standing ovation if the actors had remained paralyzed on the floor. It was the *standing up*, the undefeatable, amazing human spirit on stage, front and center, that brought the audience to its feet.

As an interesting side note, the Broadway musical closed in 1973 after only three performances. It actually sold out for the final two performances, because everyone in New York had heard how bad it was and wanted to see it before it closed. But recently—some 40 years later—it was completely reworked and revived off-Broadway. I got to see it, and loved it, as did most of the critics, and what was once heralded as "the biggest flop" is now being performed in theaters across the country. I guess that means the last word isn't always the last word.

And "Carrie" sure wasn't the last word for Betty or her career.

I hope this story will help you better understand that *Being Amazing* is not really a destination; it's more a way of life. Betty Buckley is an amazing actress, performer, and mentor, but it's her commitment to facing challenges head-on and her willingness to get up after a setback that has earned her a place in my *Amazing Hall of Fame*. As I write this, Betty, at age 71, is just beginning a national tour of *Hello, Dolly!*, and I am looking forward to seeing her when the tour gets to the Northeast!

Question: What can I do with the negative voices in my head, and how can I learn to replace them with more positive ones?

Another great question! If you think I say that a lot, it's because I am so excited that you're with me on this journey and often even one step ahead! Most of us have those voices in our head, and we may never get them to go away completely. But what we can do is add other more positive voices in our head, and eventually the negative ones will begin to diminish. Here are some things you can do.

Every time you hear that negative voice, take the message and flip it. If you hear, "Who do you think you are to be following this ridiculous dream?" flip it and say out loud, "I am so glad I'm finding my self-confidence and moving through my goals!" We do know that our minds tend to simply listen and react to messages. Your job is to create new messages to counter the negative ones and eventually *outnumber* the negative ones! Don't just do this for yourself. Do it for your family and friends and even your coworkers, too. It's actually a fun process, and you'll not only be helping others, but they may one day soon return the favor.

Question: Wow, sometimes I feel like you're reading my mind. Are there other things you think I should expect or know about?

Well, there's one thing we haven't talked much about, and that's how the *becoming amazing* journey is so much fun.

When we're living lives that are connected to our passions and our purpose, things seem to go a lot more smoothly. When our daily actions are aligned with our *spirit blueprint*, change is easier, we're more resilient, and we tend to be happier, more creative, more effective, less frustrated, and generally less stressed. The more time we spend *doing* rather than *dreaming*, the more we discover that what we used to call "work" becomes "fun." And if you have to work for a while doing something you don't love as a stepping-stone to making something you do love a bigger part of your life, then even that work becomes easier to bear.

Question: We also haven't talked about how our plan to *Be Amazing* will impact those around us—the positive, the negative, and the wonderful. How we can help others to *Be Amazing*, too?

As you embark on your *Be Amazing* journey, you will inspire some around you to pursue their own dreams, but you may discover that others feel threatened. After all, you're changing, and change is generally difficult for all of us, and especially difficult for those who are standing still. Talking about your journey, sharing your excitement, and the fun you're having can help, and it can also be bothersome to, others. So be alert, pay attention to how people are reacting, and spend more time sharing your journey with folks who support and encourage you.

You do have a responsibility to be kind and respectful, but you are not expected to sell yourself short or dim your light to make others feel more comfortable.

Question: Could you give us a couple more examples of how a "Be Amazing" approach could work with other businesses?

If you have a business or a service you'd like to Be Amazing, the principles and steps I've described will work just as well for you, too. As you begin to identify what your amazing business could look like, it will be essential to consider what "Be Amazing" might look and feel like from your customers' perspective.

Southwest Airlines is one of my favorite examples of this process. I suspect they launched many of their trademark practices by looking at things from the customers' perspective. I'd be willing to bet they spent time uncovering what travelers don't like about air travel. And I bet they put themselves in the customers' place and asked themselves what they'd love to see done differently. What are the practices we could embrace that would make our airline stand out? And what could we do to be amazing? Here are some of the things I like about Southwest, and I bet I am not alone.

First of all, making changes in travel plans on Southwest is as easy as it gets, and making a change or even canceling a flight doesn't cost a dime. If your travel plans change, Southwest has your back. If you can be flexible, they also make it easy for you to find the best fares available. Their online tool shows all the fares and flight schedules around your travel dates, allowing you to easily compare prices to check for days with lower fares. And the last thing that comes to mind is their "bags fly free" policy. Almost every airline I know charges an extra fee. Southwest has decided to let you check two bags and a carry-on item without any additional charge. When you take these practices and add a friendly and often hilarious staff, they've created an amazing travel experience.

Another example that comes to mind, because my son works there, is Lakeland Regional Health Medical Center in Lakeland, Florida. Hospitals and healthcare in general are complicated businesses, and if you want to be an amazing hospital, you have to look at many different aspects of your operations. Dr. Elaine Thompson, the President and CEO of Lakeland Regional Hospital, decided that she wanted to run an amazing hospital, so she and her team began looking at areas they could address. One area that almost everyone in the healthcare industry struggles with is emergency room care. Elaine knew there were three major emergency room concerns: quality care, wait time, and patient safety.

Elaine's team asked themselves how they could re-create an emergency room that would address these concerns in new and innovative ways. They knew that to be amazing they would have to shake things up and approach providing ER services from a new vantage point. Janet Fansler, the Executive VP and Chief Nurse, took charge of the redesign, and staff began to rethink how patients could be admitted, evaluated, and cared for. One key focus area was the physical space, and their team developed a total service redesign with patient comfort, less waiting, and timely access to exceptional care being the desired outcomes.

LRH has the busiest emergency department in the entire country and one of the best, too. Today, 80 percent of the patients that come through their emergency room doors are examined by a physician and discharged, or they are admitted to a medical floor within 180 minutes. And healthcare

administrators from many states and even other countries regularly visit Elaine and her team to see how LRH developed an amazing ER service that improves care, focuses on the customer experience, and drastically lowers wait times.

Question: Since you mentioned your son, now I'm wondering . . . how do we teach our kids that they have the potential to *Be Amazing* and show them how to develop a *Be Amazing* mind-set?

This is an easy one! You *teach* through your *actions*. Encouraging your kids to eat healthy foods while you eat potato chips and donuts is not going to work. You teach children to follow their dreams by following your own dreams. It's that simple and that profound! If you are not living the life you want, then you are not teaching *them* to live the life you want them to have. At the moment, you may be working at a job that's not ideal in order to pay the bills, but you are showing your children that things don't always come easy and that hard work and sometimes doing things we don't like are just a part of life. But it's so important to find small ways to pursue your dreams. In this way you're teaching them that dreams count, and not giving up on your dreams means everything.

Question: Could you circle back to the *Be Amazing* qualities and remind me how they relate to all we have been doing?

It seems like such a long time ago that we spoke of these qualities, and you're right; it does make sense to circle back. When I look back at all the stories I have shared with you, I am reminded that over and over, these qualities showed up in so many unique and beautiful ways. Did you notice them, too? Here they are again in all their glory to guide you on your journey to *amazing:*

Be Amazing Quality One: Offer unexpected acts of generosity, kindness, and other thoughtful behaviors.
Remember that unanticipated and complimentary giant pancake appetizer at The Maple Counter Cafe way back when we first started this amazing journey together? Never underestimate the power of a first impression. Even the smallest of efforts can make someone feel appreciated or valued. In fact, it could be more impactful than you ever imagine!

Be Amazing Quality Two: Don't necessarily strive for being the best, but do strive to be the very best you can be.
I am sure Kory and Rachel are always looking for opportunities to improve their restaurant, and growing, adapting, and improving are what makes our journey engaging and fun. Perfection simply isn't possible, and who really wants the stress of trying to be perfect, anyway? But if you put your heart and soul into everything you do, you will naturally rise to any occasion that reaches its hand out to greet you.

***Be Amazing Quality Three: Have an intention that becomes
a narrative—even if it's only one sentence long.***
At The Maple Counter Cafe, they strove to create a space that
"smiles on the world." Consider what your spirit blueprint is
and then think about the first steps you can take to breathe life
into it. Consider writing it down so that you will have a guiding principle or a mission that will help propel you forward.

Be Amazing Quality Four: Be as accommodating as possible.
You'll remember we had to wait for a table at The Maple
Counter Cafe. But we were made to feel attended to and
appreciated. They went out of their way to cater to our needs
and make us all feel like we were their top priority! Even when
things don't always go as planned, putting in just a little extra
effort can help with any bump in the road.

***Be Amazing Quality Five: Create a community, serve the one
you're in, or bring disparate communities together.***
At the end of the day, all we truly want is to feel that we *belong*.
When we create opportunities for connection, like the Maple
Counter Cafe Sunday night get-togethers, the hidden gifts
that bubble to the surface can be immeasurable. Our communities can also blossom into makeshift *families* that provide
much-needed support at a moment's notice.

I'm not going to lie or pretend that this process isn't
without its challenges or that it will always be easy. *Being
Amazing* requires a plan, takes courage, and involves a lot
of hard work, too. (Which explains why everyone around
you isn't making something amazing happen right now!)
But that's also why you've been working on a plan that's so

important and life-changing. You are discovering you're braver than you thought, and that hard work isn't going to stand in your way and stop you from making your dreams come true.

You know it's not easy. But at the end of the day, you do have time for *one small step.* You've learned that having courage doesn't mean you aren't scared; it just means you're not going to let being scared stop you. And you've figured out that hard work isn't impossible—it's just *hard work.* As you take those small steps and push through the fear and the hard work, you'll discover a renewed energy slowly bubbling back up in your life. You'll also soon meet your two new best friends, "Enthusiasm" and "Excitement"! And then, slowly but surely, all that hard work begins to feel so much lighter and more like a good and productive workout that propels you closer and closer to your amazing dream.

Remember, you have a *choice.* You can sit on the couch and watch another sitcom, or you can be like Susan, who began writing poetry while getting her chemo treatments and will soon complete her soulful collection of poems. You can be like Edward, who tirelessly works two jobs but sits in front of his computer for fifteen minutes every night before bed, chasing his dream to learn Spanish so he can move to Madrid. Or, you can be like Ryan, who was our postman for three years while he studied architecture at night school. He just started his dream job with an architectural firm he's been eyeing for almost two years. Or you could be like ninety-one-year-old Helen, who fell in her kitchen two winters ago and was confined to her floor for twenty-four hours before she was found, all because she couldn't reach her cell phone. Before long, she and a friend opened an ETSY store selling beautiful quilted, wearable cell phone holders.

You begin *where* you are, with *what* you have, and then you take that very first small step. Then you are already one step closer than you were before. Remember, every book began with a single sentence. And every garden started with just a few seeds.

If Susan and Edward and Ryan and Helen and so many others who are busy making their dreams come true can do it, you can, too.

I must admit, as we prepare to wrap up our time together, I'm feeling a bit emotional thinking about you as you set out on your own unique and beautiful amazing journey. But before we part, there are just a few closing thoughts I'd like to share and hope you'll revisit this section from time to time, especially when you need some encouragement or inspiration.

Sometimes, when I am at a concert, I turn away from the performance or performer and look at the *audience* instead. I take in the faces all around me, the expressions, the smiles, the joy and goodwill unfolding right before me in this beautiful, shared experience, and I remember that we are all connected in some cosmic, brilliant, mysterious way. I am feeling this right now, and I am excited and confident that soon you will be making your amazing dreams a reality.

So please remember . . .

You were born *amazing*. You were born with the potential to do amazing things, and you were born to share your amazingness with the world. You have a unique spirit blueprint that is a gift and also a responsibility. If some of the challenges of life have gotten in the way or sent you on an unexpected detour in finding the road back to your core essence and spirit blueprint, don't despair! You can recover and reclaim it *right now*.

Imagine that there is a small gate in front of you and listen carefully, because you are being called to open it and step into a beautiful, forgotten garden. This garden will be instantly familiar, because you have dreamt about it over and over for a very long time. You will remember it, because you use to play there every day, and everything is exactly as you left it such a long time ago.

And although *Being Amazing* isn't really a destination, it *is* a journey meant just for you. The pathway beyond the gate will reveal itself as you take each small step forward. And what you are remembering and will one day fully realize is a sacred calling that has been in your heart this whole time. You are finally *home*, again.

As you seek *amazing*, you can start with a small goal that will just naturally evolve into other areas of your life, or you may discover what you thought was small is actually much bigger than it first appeared. Accept that your spirit blueprint has mysterious edges to it that will be revealed when the time is right and when you are ready.

Being Amazing isn't about being perfect or about getting it right every time, but it *will* require you to move beyond "good enough." *Being Amazing* is about *you* being *you*. Not the you you thought you were, but the you you were always meant to be. Remember that amazing restaurant in Walla Walla? It's *your* turn now. You get to write your story. You get to describe what *your* amazing pancake will look like, taste like, and be like, and once you know, you get to create your amazing pancake just the way it was meant to be.

And as you go . . .

Remember how powerful your thoughts are and practice reframing those thoughts in a way that lifts you up and encourages you to live your dream.

Remember to roll up those sleeves and keep taking those small steps.

Remember to ask for help when you need it and offer help to others, too.

Remember that you can't be stuck *and* moving at the same time.

Remember to acknowledge the challenges but focus on the solutions.

Remember we all get fearful and then remember healthy fear is there to protect us, not suffocate us.

Remember you don't have to wait until you're "feeling like it." Take a step and let the feelings gently catch up.

Remember not to focus on all the power you *don't* have; focus on all that you *do* have.

Remember to seek out the people who inspire you and then inspire those people you're around.

And if you remember nothing else, always remember to be grateful, to be kind, and to smile often, because you are here, like all of us, to simply *Be Amazing.*

Acknowledgments

First to my friend and mentor Mark Dagostino, who introduced me to my amazing agent Tom Flannery at AGI Literary Co. who believed in me and Be Amazing. To the folks at Skyhorse, and especially to my editor Abigail Gehring, who patiently nurtured me, and skillfully and enthusiastically brought the book to completion. To my dear friend and author Jacob Nordby, who is always the first person I call when I have a question or an idea related to books and writing and life. To Stacy Creamer who read an early draft and offered insight and advice, and Teresa Dainesi, who took a last look at the almost final manuscript and tightened things up considerably. And to Dave Bastien, the IT guru who knows how to do things I can't even begin to understand, and to my social media assistant, Jamie Barone, who makes a difference in my life every single day.

I especially want to thank my children and their partners: Josh and Rachel, Molly and Jason, and Timothy and Alvin. And my grandchildren: Grace, Andrew, Kash, and Ty. They are always there for me and are still laughing at my jokes, allowing me to think I am funnier than I really am. And to my partner, Michael, who continues to see me through rose-colored glasses and who proves there are always surprises that can change your life in wonderful ways. And

finally, to Toby dog, the champion of unconditional love and joyful living.

You are all amazing and I am very, very grateful!

About the Author

Paul S. Boynton is the author of several books including Amazon Bestseller *Begin with Yes*, around which Paul built a massive and extraordinarily engaged audience of over two million followers. A true force of nature and popular keynote speaker, Paul is also President and CEO of The Moore Center, an organization serving people with intellectual disabilities. His writing has frequently been featured in *The Huffington Post*, the *NH Business Review* and *The Good Men Project*. Paul has degrees in both social work and counseling. He lives with his partner and their dog Toby in New Hampshire and spends much of his free time visiting his three adult children and their families. Visit Paul online at www.facebook.com /beginwithyes and www.beginwithyes.com.

Book Club Discussion Questions

1. In the introduction, Paul writes, "What makes each of us unique is not a problem; it's an amazing blessing." What are some things that make you unique? Are they things you're proud of or ashamed of? Why?

2. Paul writes about the Maple Counter Cafe and what an amazing breakfast experience he had there. Can you think of an experience you've had with a person or place that felt really amazing? What was so amazing about it?

3. Are there areas in your life where you already feel amazing? Did you work at becoming amazing at those things? What did you do?

4. What are the risks in striving to be amazing at something? Are there aspects that feel scary or intimidating?

5. On pages 25–26, Paul lists common challenges holding people back from reaching for their dreams. Are there other challenges unique to you? How might you "reprogram your mind" to change your limiting beliefs?

6. Of the six *Be Amazing* qualities (pages 12–18) that Paul identifies, which ones come easily to you and which ones might require more effort?

7. Can you describe a time when simply rolling up your sleeves and doing the hard work got you through a situation that at first seemed impossibly difficult? How about a time when working harder was simply not enough?

8. In which areas might you need to ask for help to get past your roadblocks? Is it easy or hard for you to ask for help? Why?

9. Take a look at the questions related to your "spirit blueprint" on pages 47–48. Did these questions bring up anything unexpected for you? Did they help to clarify your focus?

10. If you know what you want to be amazing at, can you name a few things that would describe "amazing" for you in that role? Give others in the group a chance to share what they think would be amazing characteristics. For example, on page 60, Paul writes, "An amazing teacher would have a skill to share, would love working with others, would be excited and passionate about what she was teaching."

11. How might you help others as you begin the process of being amazing in your chosen area? Can you give someone else a hand as they strive to be amazing, too?
12. What's the difference between being accommodating to other people and becoming a doormat? Do you need to set some healthy boundaries in your life?
13. What is the first step you will take on your new journey to being amazing?

Notes

....

....

....

....

....

....

....

....

....

....

....

....

....

....

....

....

....

....

....

....

....

....

....

....

....

....

....

....

....

....

....

....

....

....

....

....

....

....

....

....

....

....

....

....

....

....

....

....

....

....

....

....